Essential
New Zealand

by
ALLAN EDIE

PASSPORT BOOKS
a division of *NTC Publishing Group*
Lincolnwood, Illinois USA

Published by Passport Books, a division of NTC Publishing Group, 4255 West Touhy Avenue, Lincolnwood (Chicago), Illinois 60646–1975 U.S.A.

The contents of this publication are believed correct at the time of printing. Nevertheless, the publishers cannot accept responsibility for errors or omissions, nor for changes in details given. We are always grateful to readers who let us know of any errors or omissions they come across, and future printings will be updated accordingly.

Published by Passport Books in conjunction with The Automobile Association of Great Britain.

Written by Allan Edie
"Peace and Quiet" section by Paul Sterry

Library of Congress Catalog
Card Number 94–68544
ISBN 0–8442–8947–7

10 9 8 7 6 5 4 3 2 1

PRINTED IN TRENTO, ITALY

Front cover picture: Mount Cook

The weather chart displayed on **page 107** of this book is calibrated in °C and millimeters. For conversion to °F and inches simply use the following formula:

$25\cdot4mm = 1$ inch $\qquad °F = 1\cdot8 \times °C + 32$

INTRODUCTION	4
BACKGROUND	6
AUCKLAND AND THE NORTHERN REGION	13
WELLINGTON AND CENTRAL NEW ZEALAND	38
SOUTH ISLAND: CHRISTCHURCH AND THE NORTH	53
DUNEDIN AND THE DEEP SOUTH	69
PEACE AND QUIET Countryside and Wildlife in New Zealand	90
FOOD AND DRINK	99
SHOPPING	101

ACCOMMODATION	103
CULTURE, ENTERTAINMENT AND NIGHTLIFE	105
WEATHER AND WHEN TO GO	106
HOW TO BE A LOCAL	108
CHILDREN	110
TIGHT BUDGET	111
SPECIAL EVENTS	112
SPORT	113
DIRECTORY	115
LANGUAGE	126
INDEX	127

Maps and Plans

New Zealand	5, 7
The Northern Region	14–15
Auckland Environs	18-19
Northland	26
Central New Zealand	40–41
Wellington	44–45
Christchurch Environs	56–57
South Island: The North	64–65
Dunedin Environs	70–71
The Deep South	74–75

This book employs a simple rating system to help choose which places to visit:

✓	'top ten'

◆◆◆	do not miss
◆◆	see if you can
◆	worth seeing if you have time

INTRODUCTION

'The World in Miniature' is a description often applied to the 'Down-Under' country of New Zealand. On a globe of the world it seems to occupy such a small space in the South Pacific, but scenically, with its variety and beauty, it can match any bigger or more famous country.

From the tip of the North Island to the southernmost extremity of the South, New Zealand is only 1,100 miles (1,770km), yet within this compact area are mountains above 10,000 feet (3,000m), volcanoes – dead and alive, hot springs and geysers, glaciers and fiords.

New Zealand's seeming remoteness from the more populous parts of the world has created an inventive independence in its people's spirit. This small nation – of less than 3.5 million population today – has fielded more than its share of heroes, from Sir Edmund Hillary, conqueror of Everest to Lord Ernest Rutherford, pioneer of atomic research.

New Zealand shares all the technological and economic benefits of modern western affluence, yet one of its most redeeming features is the ease with which you can leave the 20th century behind, and get away from it all – on a secluded beach, or exploring the thick of a forest, or skiing on a high snowfield, or tramping a lowland valley. For some of New Zealand remains in the original natural state of a thousand, or perhaps even ten thousand years ago.

You can come face to face with nature, but so compact is the country, you can have a motor-home close by, an airport not too far away and the luxuries of modern towns and hotels within reach.

Urban New Zealand, too, has a relaxed lifestyle. Even its largest city, Auckland, has a population of less than a million, and handsome Wellington, the capital, on its fine bay, is more like a flourishing seaside resort than a London or Washington. Recently New Zealand has capitalised on this fact by promoting itself nostalgically as being the way life used to be.

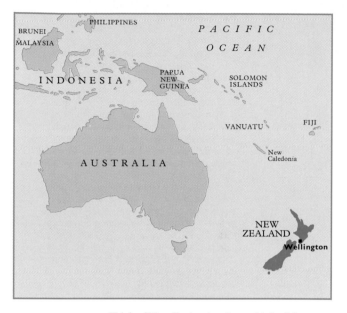

Think of New Zealand and you think of sheep
… In some country areas, the scene can have
changed little in a hundred years, as sheep
farmers (admittedly, sometimes on
motorcycles) gather their flocks with the help
of dogs, and professional shearers travel from
farm to farm to exercise their skill. Wool and
mutton have long been vital to New Zealand's
economy, and even today, sheep outnumber
people by 19 to one.

New Zealand is not a sophisticated country. It
has been suggested that rugby, racing and
beer sum up its culture and, certainly, sport is
almost a religion. Football and horse racing
are avidly followed, and most New
Zealanders, if they are not players, are at
least followers of sporting events. This applies
most of all to males, and it is perhaps as a
corollary to it that sexism is an attitude that
undoubtedly exists. However, 'Kiwis' – as
New Zealanders like to call themselves after
their endearing national bird – are at the
same time unusually friendly and hospitable
towards visitors.

BACKGROUND

In the South Pacific Ocean about midway between the Equator and the South Pole, New Zealand is a country of around 104,000 square miles (269,000 sq km) – roughly the same size as Great Britain or Italy, or just two-thirds the size of California.

It is divided into two main islands – North Island and South Island. In the far south, Stewart Island – only 675 square miles (1,750 sq km) – is the third island and there are also other smaller islands, with little population. The South Island is slightly larger in area than the North, and its inhabitants delight in referring to it as the mainland. In terms of population and commerce, the North is the premier island, but it is beaten into second place by the South, not just in land area, but also by the scenic beauty that land area contains. The 45th parallel bisects the South Island, and the country lies close to the 180th meridian, along which is situated the International Dateline. Consequently, New Zealand is one of the first countries to see each new day, sitting as it does, twelve hours ahead of GMT.

The Land

Up to 70 million years ago, New Zealand was part of a large landmass including Australia and Antarctica. When this split up, New Zealand drifted away to its position of isolation, more than 1,000 miles (1,600km) southeast of its closest neighbour, Australia, and a unique flora and fauna developed.

Lack of predators led to the evolution of flightless birds such as the kiwi, the takahe and the extinct moa. The earth underlying New Zealand is unstable, and the land is marked by volcanic activity. Auckland is built on a series of extinct volcanoes, there are active and dormant volcanoes throughout the North Island, and the popular resort of Rotorua is famous for its geysers and hot springs.

The terrain is rugged, with ranges of hills and mountains running through both islands. Over 75 per cent of the land is above 650 feet (200m) in altitude; there are over 220 named

NEW ZEALAND

North Cape
Kaitaia
Kaikohe
Dargaville
Whangarei
Great Barrier I.
Coromandel Peninsula
Auckland Manukau
Coromandel
Thames
NORTH
ISLAND
Hamilton
Bay of
Plenty
Tasman
Whakatane
Te Kuiti
Rotorua
Sea
Gisborne
Taupo
New Plymouth
Lake
Taupo
Wairoa
Cape Egmont
Mt. Ruapehu
Napier
2518m
3797m
Hawke Bay
Hastings
Wanganui
Dannevirke
Cape Farewell
D'Urville
Palmerston
I.
Levin
North
Tasman
Bay
Motueka
Masterton
Cook Strait
Nelson
Picton
Lower Hutt
SOUTH
Westport
Blenheim
Wellington
ISLAND
Reefton
2338m
Greymouth
Kaikoura
Hokitika
Southern Alps
Mt. Cook
Pegasus Bay
3764m
Christchurch
Ashburton
Banks Peninsula
Canterbury Bight
3027m
Waitaki
Timaru
P A C I F I C
Queenstown
Te Anau
Wakatipu
Oamaru
L.
Te Anau
Clutha
West
O C E A N
Cape
Dunedin
Balclutha
Foveaux Strait
Invercargill
Stewart
Strait
Island

0   200   400km
0   100   200 miles

peaks rising above 7,500 feet (2,300m), the highest being Mount Cook in the Southern Alps, with a peak of 12,349 feet (3,763m). The undulating topography gives rise to a number of big rivers, which in turn have provided abundant hydro-electric power. The Waikato River, the longest at 220 miles (354km), has nine dams on it; and its waters are also used for cooling by three thermal power plants.

The influential Maori chief Hongi Hika, on his deathbed, counsels peace with the missionaries in 1828

The New Zealand forest, known as 'bush', provides a lush evergreen cladding. In most cases the rich pasturelands, which are now also an important aspect of the land, were won from the bush by much sweat and toil. The climate is not extreme. Temperatures are higher in the north, and rainfall greater to the west of the mountains.

The Past
The Maoris
The first human beings arrived in New Zealand about 1,000 years ago from eastern Polynesia. The Maoris trace their history, through folklore and legend, back to a heavenly land they call 'Hawaiki', this may, in reality, have been the Society Islands or the Cook Islands northeast of New Zealand. Legend identifies the Polynesian discoverer of New Zealand as Kupe, who came around AD950, followed by Toi 200 years later. Around 1350, according to tradition, a great fleet of canoes arrived, and to the present day Maoris trace their tribal origins to ancestors arriving on one or other of these canoes. Archaeologists and anthropologists suggest there were two periods of Maori culture. The Archaic period was possibly established soon after AD1000 with nomadic hunters and gatherers following food – often the now

extinct giant moa – and having few permanent villages. In the later, Classic period of Maori culture there were permanent villages, fortifications (*pa*) and cultivation.

Tribal life ordained the Maori social system, regulated by priests (*tohunga*) and chiefs (*rangitira*). There was a stringent warrior code. Tribes often fought with other tribes, and revenge for any slight was an important ritual, though it might go back generations.

The Coming of the *Pakeha*

The first white man to see New Zealand was probably the Dutchman Abel Tasman in 1642. He sailed the west coast and named the land Staten Landt. The name was soon changed to Nieuw Zeeland. It was not until 1769 that the English navigator Captain James Cook stepped ashore. He was the first to circumnavigate both main islands, and visited New Zealand three times. Generally, he had amicable dealings with the Maoris. It was largely Cook's reports of the new country that brought the next wave of people.

Whalers and traders of various nationalities came in their boatloads, the whalers to harpoon the whales running the coast and the traders to purchase flax (for rope), kauri tree spars, and even impaled Maori heads. Often, the payment would be in guns. The possession of firearms enabled some Maori tribes to do battle like never before and it is estimated that about 60,000 died in inter-tribal warfare during the early years of the 19th century. Diseases like influenza were brought by the Europeans and these also killed many Maoris. It is thought that the Maoris numbered somewhere between 100,000 and 200,000 when the Europeans – or 'Pakeha' as the Maoris called them – first arrived. By 1896, there were only 42,000. In the wake of the sailors and merchants came the missionaries, spreading Christianity in all its forms, and then the settlers.

British Rule

In 1833, with the threat of French annexation of New Zealand, the British government posted Australian civil servant James Busby there as

'British Resident'. In 1839 Captain William Hobson, who was named lieutenant-governor by the British government, annexed the North Island by right of cession and the South Island by right of discovery. In 1840, he was authorised to sign an accord with Maori leaders and offer them the rights and privileges of subjects of Queen Victoria. The Treaty of Waitangi transferred the sovereignty of New Zealand to Britain and guaranteed the Maori people possession of their lands. The treaty was perhaps vague in some of its wording (the Maori and English versions differ) and still today remains a confusing document.

The pace of settlement increased from the 1840s, and by the late 1850s, European settlers outnumbered Maoris. Migrant schemes brought out settlers from England and Scotland, though there were also immigrants from France, Bohemia (now in Czech and Slovak Republics), Dalmatia (now in Croatia) and Scandinavia. Land for settlement was purchased from the Maoris with a combination of money and bartered goods, but there were misunderstandings over what was actually being traded in land sales and soon the Maoris became alarmed at the amount of land they were losing. There were skirmishes between Maori and Pakeha in areas near the Bay of Islands, Blenheim, New Plymouth, and Wanganui, and in 1864 a 'land war' was fought by British troops and local volunteers against the Waikato Maori in the area immediately south of Auckland. There were three or four battles which were finally won by the Pakeha, and much of the land of the Waikato Maoris was confiscated by the Government.

The discovery of gold in the 1860s brought people from all over the world, but it was a short-lived bonanza, over by the 1870s. New Zealand's economy sank into depression, but encouragement for farmers – particularly in sheep – led to a recovery. Under a Liberal government, some radical social legislation was passed, including votes for women in 1893 and the introduction of non-contributory old age pensions in 1898 – two world 'firsts'.

On Milford Sound, 'the eighth wonder of the world'

Independent New Zealand

By the beginning of the 20th century, second-generation New Zealanders of European extraction were acquiring a pride in themselves and their country. This patriotism was enhanced by the performance of New Zealand soldiers who supported Great Britain in the Boer War and two World Wars – with great losses. In 1907, New Zealand had acquired Dominion status and in 1931 gained full autonomy under the Statute of Westminster, although it was not until 1947 that the right, under the Statute, to amend the country's constitution, was finally exercised. During the second half of the 20th century, political power alternated btween the National Party – traditionally the party of farming, business and affluent urban dwellers – and the Labour Party – originally the party of the workers.

In the 1980s, under a Labour government, New Zealand took an independent stance, in the world community, on defence and nuclear weapons – for instance, warships carrying nuclear weapons were banned from entering New Zealand harbours. The National Party government, which took power in 1990, continued the no-nuclear policy.

New Zealand Today

New Zealand's population today is around 3.35 million, 75 per cent of whom live in the North Island – and nearly one million of those in the greater Auckland area. About 84 per cent are Pakeha, mainly of English or Scottish ancestry. There are about 275,000 (9 per cent of the population) with Maori or part-Maori

BACKGROUND

'Sheep may safely graze': a pastoral view of New Zealand

blood. There are also about 100,000 Polynesians, mainly from the South Pacific islands of Samoa, Tonga, and the Cook Islands. There has also been a measure of Asian immigration.

Most New Zealanders are Christian – principally Anglican, Presbyterian, Roman Catholic and Methodist. There are Maori versions of Christianity: the Ratana and Ringatu churches. There is religious freedom and many faiths and religions are represented, though relatively few New Zealanders are 'active' followers of their religion.

Everyone over 18 has a vote to elect members to the one-chamber House of Representatives every three years. The majority party forms the government and the Cabinet is the executive body. The British monarch is the formal head of state, represented by a governor-general.

A pastoral background still underwrites the New Zealand economy, with meat, wool and dairy products being major exports. But the service industries and secondary manufacturing are now also important – so too is tourism.

Though in many ways out of the mainstream of western society with its many disorders, by the 1980s New Zealand had its fair share of such social problems as divorce, one-parent families, illegitimacy and sexual and racial disadvantage. Maori nationalism has rekindled feelings of injustice over land losses by Maoris in the 19th century after the signing of the Treaty of Waitangi.

In 1993 a Mixed Member Proportional parliamentary system was voted in – to take effect in 1996.

AUCKLAND AND THE NORTHERN REGION

From the lonely tip of Cape Reinga in the far north, where the ancient Maori spirits of the dead left New Zealand to return to their Polynesian home, to the tourist hotbed of Rotorua with its geysers, boiling mud and Maori cultural displays, this section of the North Island encompasses a variety of landscapes and experiences. The sand dunes of the Ninety Mile Beach form a mini-Sahara in the narrow peninsula at the northern extreme of North Island, known as Northland, while the Bay of Islands on the east coast, with its semi-tropical beaches, is a busy resort area, popular with divers, fishermen and sailors as well as mere sun-worshippers.

Traces of New Zealand as it was before man's arrival can be seen in the remnants of great forests of gigantic and ancient kauri trees in the northwest, and in wilderness country in the mountainous interior of the Coromandel Peninsula in the east.

A more tamed landscape characterises the middle of the North Island, where fertile plains around the Waikato River support dairy herds and agriculture. And the summer playground of the Bay of Plenty, sometimes advertised as the Orchard Coast, is – as this suggests – famous for growing fruit, sub-tropical exotica such as tamarillos and kiwifruit, as well as more familiar citrus fruits.

Other sights in the region include a lake in a volcanic crater, Lake Taupo; a cave lit by glow worms, Waitomo Cave; and New Zealand's largest city, Auckland.

AUCKLAND

With a population of nearly one million, Auckland is home to more than a quarter of all New Zealanders. About 20 per cent are Pacific Islanders, making Auckland the world's biggest Polynesian city.

It is the main gateway for international tourists, being the principal port for passenger ships on line voyages and cruises, and has the country's leading airport. There are air, rail, and coach services to most parts of the North Island. The city is situated at the narrowest part of the North Island, between two harbours, in places only about a mile (1.6km) apart. The Waitemata harbour, on the eastern (Pacific) side, leads out to a gulf with a number of islands. Its yacht-filled waters give Auckland one of its nicknames – City of Sails. The coathanger-shaped bridge spanning the harbour is a city landmark. The airport is on the

Maori woodcarver at work

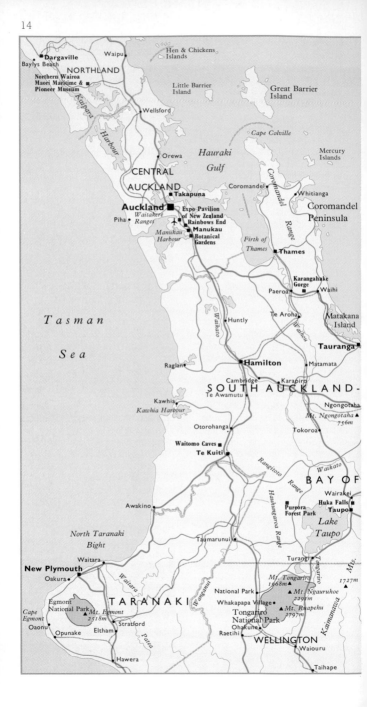

THE NORTHERN REGION

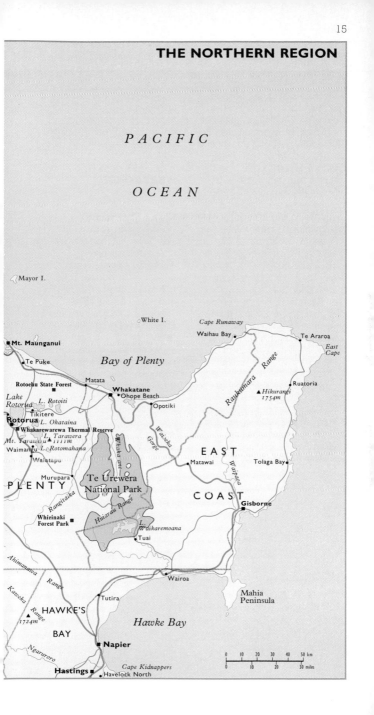

PACIFIC

OCEAN

Mayor I.

○ White I.

Cape Runaway

Waihau Bay

Te Araroa

East Cape

■ **Mt. Maunganui**

Te Puke

Bay of Plenty

Raukumara Range

Rotoehu State Forest

Matata

Whakatane ■

Hikurangi 1754m ▲

Ruatoria

Lake Rotorua

L. Rotoiti

Ohope Beach

Opotiki

Wattoha Gorge

Rotorua ■

Tikitere

L. Okataina

L. Tarawera

Mt. Tarawera ▲ 1111m

Waimangu L. Rotomahana

Waiotapu

Murupara

Whakarewarewa Thermal Reserve ■

EAST

Matawai

Waipaoa

Tolaga Bay

Te Urewera National Park

P L E N T Y

Rangitaika

C O A S T

Huiarau Range

Gisborne ●

Whirinaki Forest Park ■

L. Waikaremoana

Tuai ●

Ahimanawa Range

Wairoa

Kaweka Range

Mahia Peninsula

HAWKE'S

Tutira

▲ 1724m

Hawke Bay

BAY

Ngaruroro

■ **Napier**

0 10 20 30 40 50 km

Hastings ■

Cape Kidnappers

0 10 20 30 miles

Havelock North ●

THE NORTHERN REGION

shores of the second harbour, the Manukau, on the Tasman Sea side of Auckland's neck of land. Less commercial than the Waitemata harbour, it is a good area for birdwatchers. Past geological turbulence has shaped the city's setting. As many as 48 extinct volcanoes dot the city area, making it gently hilly, with a number of peaks offering viewpoints. The last volcano to erupt – 600 years ago – was Rangitoto, on an island inside the Waitemata harbour, and visible from many parts of the city.

The downtown area is compact, but beyond it Auckland sprawls in a succession of subsidiary cities and suburbs. Auckland's sights are also spread out, making car an ideal means of sightseeing. There are separate morning and afternoon tours by bus, and also an hourly tourist service, the United Airlines Explorer, 10.00–17.00 hrs (on the hour). Tickets can be

Auckland from Mount Eden

obtained from the driver. This links Victoria Markets, Oriental Markets, Mission Bay, Underwater World, the Rose Gardens, Museum and Parnell Village.

WHAT TO SEE

◆
CITY ART GALLERY
Wellesley Street East
The gallery stands on the edge of Albert Park, one of Auckland's many green areas. It houses an important collection of New Zealand art of the past and present, as well as European Old Masters and a collection of prints and drawings. Travelling exhibitions from abroad are often to be seen here. The gallery itself is a Victorian structure once threatened with demolition. *Open*: 10.00–17.00hrs. Admission free.

◆◆
DOMAIN AND MUSEUM
These extensive parklands

covering some 200 acres (80 hectares), about a mile (1.6km) from downtown, contain a museum, gardens and a tropical winterhouse.

The **War Memorial Museum,** on the top of the Domain's volcano, not only has a military display, but also exhibits on Maori culture, colonial life, animals, birds and fish of New Zealand and the art of the South Pacific.

Museum open: daily 10.00–17.00hrs.

◆
EXPO PAVILION OF NEW ZEALAND
Montgomerie Road
Situated just about a mile (1.6km) from Auckland Airport, this recreates the acclaimed New Zealand exhibit at the 1988 World Expo in Brisbane, Australia. Shows illustrating the culture and geography of New Zealand start every half hour.
Open: daily 09.00–17.00hrs.

◆◆◆
KELLY TARLTON'S UNDERWATER WORLD ✓

Tamaki Drive, Orakei
This large aquarium displays marine animals, including moray eels, kingfish and sharks, all from in and around New Zealand. The aquarium is underground, and visitors are carried past the large tanks on a pedestrian conveyor in a transparent tunnel. You can step off the moving walkway on to a footpath alongside if you want a longer look at any

One of Auckland's yellow pedicabs

creature. Such close proximity to the animals gives the illusion of being at the bottom of the sea.

New Zealand's fish are not colourful, but nevertheless the exhibit is unusual and well done. There is a theatre with an audio-visual show, displays of shells and a souvenir shop. There is also the **Antarctic Encounter** which offers an underground ride with 'Antarctic' special effects.
Open: daily 09.00–21.00hrs. Admission charge.

◆◆◆
MOUNT EDEN AND ONE TREE HILL
From Mount Eden, highest of Auckland's volcanic peaks at 541 feet (165m), there is a

THE NORTHERN REGION

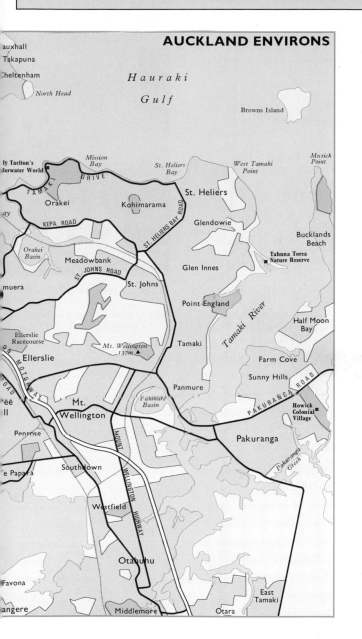

AUCKLAND ENVIRONS

spectacular view over the city's central areas and the main harbour. The top is reached by road, about 2½ miles (4km) from downtown.

Outside the crater are traces of an ancient Maori fortress. **One Tree Hill** situated 3½ miles (6km) out of the town centre, in Cornwall Park, also offers fine views. The original 'one tree' was planted in the 17th century. There is now a single pine on top – and an obelisk.

◆

MUSEUM OF TRANSPORT AND TECHNOLOGY
Great North Road, Western Springs
MOTAT, as it is known, is three miles (5km) west of downtown. It houses a big display of yesteryear nostalgia: old cars and trams, aeroplanes (including a re-creation of New Zealand's first), printing machinery and a re-created colonial village.
Open: Monday to Friday 09.00–17.00hrs, weekends and holidays 10.00–17.00hrs.

◆

ZOO
Motions Road, Western Springs
The zoo is linked to the Museum of Transport and Technology by an electric tram service.
Exotic and local animals are kept here in spacious surroundings. New Zealand's symbolic bird, the kiwi, is well displayed.
Open: daily 09.30–17.30hrs. Admission charge.

Lounging on the beach at Devonport

Bush, Beaches and Islands
If you want to get out of the city for a few hours, there are plenty of short trips you can take. The largest area of bush – native forest – is the Waitakere Ranges situated about nine miles (15km) to the west of the city. The **Waitakere Scenic Drive** goes through the Centennial Memorial Park (15,800 acres/6,400 hectares) established in 1940. There are 135 named tracks in the ranges, some of them offering easy walking. Auckland has a large number and variety of beaches in its greater area.

Mission Bay on Tamaki Drive is one of the closest to downtown – about 2½ miles (4km). Over the Waitemata harbour bridge the suburb of **Takapuna** hugs its pleasant shoreline, while at **Orewa**, 18 miles (30km) north, a two-mile (3km) long beach

offers great family outings. Surfers would prefer **Piha**, where the waves roll in to the black sands of the west coast. Piha is 25 miles (40km) west of downtown, via the Waitakere Ranges.

Ferries leave the Ferry berth at the bottom of Queen Street for 10-minute trips to the North Shore suburb of Devonport. There are also a number of cruises on the Waitemata Harbour and to the islands of the Hauraki Gulf (45 minutes or longer). You can visit Rangitoto Island, rich in life despite the relatively recent eruption, and others of the 47 islands in the Hauraki Gulf Maritime Park that are not wildlife reserves.

From Mechanics Bay, just a mile (1.6km) from the Ferry berth, small amphibious planes and helicopters offer scenic flights over the city, harbour and gulf. If time does not permit you to see much of Auckland's marine

areas, then at least take the Tamaki Drive along the waterfront past Kelly Tarlton's Underworld World to Mission Bay.

Other Attractions
Aotea Centre: concert and conference centre with exhibition areas, restaurants and bars, completed 1990, on Aotea Square, Queen Street.
Botanical Gardens: 158 acres (64 hectares) of horticultural displays and walks, with information, situated 15 miles (24km) south, at Hill Road, Manurewa.
Open: daily 09.00–17.00hrs.
Howick Colonial Village: a re-creation of colonial life at Lloyd Elsmore Park, Bells Road, Pakuranga, 12½ miles (20km) east of downtown.
Open: daily 10.00–16.00hrs.
Rainbows End: family amusement and adventure park, adjacent to Manukau City centre, 13 miles (22km) south.
Open: daily in summer holidays 10.00–21.00hrs, winter Fridays 10.00–17.00hrs; and weekends 10.00–20.00hrs

Accommodation
There is a wide variety of accommodation, with hotels, motor inns, motels, and guesthouses. (Area code: 09). The following are in the upper expense bracket:
Auckland Airport Travelodge, Ascot Road, Mangere (tel: 275 1059). 243 rooms, first class; one mile (1.6km) from airport, shuttle bus.
Auckland City Travelodge, 96 Quay Street, downtown (tel: 377 0349). 188 rooms, first class;

THE NORTHERN REGION

The Regent of Auckland

next to city air terminal.
Centra, 128 Albert Street, downtown (tel: 302 1111). 256 rooms, good business hotel.
Hyatt Auckland, Princes Street, downtown (tel: 366 1234). 275 rooms, deluxe; up a hill from main street.
Pan Pacific, Mayoral Drive, downtown (tel: 366 3000). 286 rooms, 3 restaurants, deluxe.
Regent of Auckland, Albert Street, central (tel: 309 8888). 332 rooms, deluxe, Auckland's top hotel.
Sheraton Auckland, 83 Symonds Street, uptown (tel: 379 5132). 407 rooms, deluxe, including 'Towers'; half a mile (1km) from downtown.

Less expensive but of good standard are:

Barrycourt Motor Inn, 10–20 Gladstone Road, Parnell (tel: 303 3789). 11 rooms; one mile (1.6km) out, Best Western.
Kingsgate Logan Park, 187 Campbell Road, One Tree Hill (tel: 634 1269). 222 rooms; suburban, half way to airport.
Quality Inn Rose Park, 100 Gladstone Road, Parnell (tel: 377 3619). 112 rooms; one mile (1.6km) east from downtown.

For those on a budget:
Ascot Parnell, 36 St Stephen Avenue, Parnell (tel: 309 9012). One mile (1.6km) east of city centre. Provides characterful nine-room guesthouse accommodation in restored historic home.
Aspen Lodge, 62 Emily Place, central, half a mile (1km) east of main street (tel: 379 6698). 30 beds, budget bed and breakfast.
Auckland Central Backpackers, 9 Fort Street, downtown (tel: 358 4877). 144 rooms and a restaurant.
Auckland YMCA, Pitt Street, uptown (tel: 303 2068). 131 rooms, budget, half a mile (1km) west of main street.
Harbourview Station, 131 Beach Road, central, half a mile (1km) east of main street (tel: 303 2463). 70 rooms, opposite main rail station.
North Shore Caravan Park, 52 Northcote Road, Takapuna (tel: 418 2578). 2½ miles (4km) over harbour bridge, campsites and cabins.
Takapuna Beach Motor Camp, 22 The Promenade, Takapuna (tel: 489 7909). 3½ miles (6km) over harbour bridge, campsites and on-site vans.

Restaurants

Most restaurants in these listings are licensed to supply wine with a meal, though some New Zealand restaurants are 'BYO' (bring your own – a much cheaper option).

Nearly all the listed hotels have restaurants, with the Hyatt, in particular, being noted for its high standard.

Antoines, 33 Parnell Road, one mile (1.6km) from downtown; top class French cuisine.

BNZ Tower, Queen Street, downtown; light lunch food bars in basement.

Chase Plaza, Queen Street, downtown; light lunch food bars 4th floor.

Cin Cin, Ferry Building, 99 Quay Street, downtown; popular café style.

Harbourside, Ferry Building, Quay Street, downtown; first class, popular.

Hunting Lodge, Waikoukou Valley Road, Waimauku; overlooking vineyards.

Jurgens, Wyndham Street, central, top class New Zealand and European cuisine.

Langtons, on slopes of Mount Eden; buffet smorgasbord, good views.

Number Five, 5 City Road, uptown opposite the Sheraton; top class European cuisine.

Restaurant 360, 501 Karhngahape Road, uptown; revolving, buffet dining.

Sails, Westhaven Marina, one mile (1.6km) out; seafood with marine views.

Spalato, 417 Manukau Road, Epsom, five miles (8km) out of town; first class European cuisine.

Tony's Lord Nelson, Victoria Street, downtown; moderate-priced streak house.

Top of the Town, Hyatt Auckland Hotel; top standard and prices; views.

Ethnic

Ariake, Lower Albert Street, central; Japanese.

La Trattoria, 259 Parnell Road, Parnell, one mile (1.6km) out; Italian.

Mai Thai, 57 Victoria Street, west central; Thai.

Mekong, 295 Queen Street, midtown; Vietnamese.

New Orient, Strand Arcade, Queen Street, midtown; Chinese.

McDonalds, **Kentucky Fried** and **Pizza Hut** are at many locations in the city. There are many other restaurants of note.

Entertainment and Nightlife

Sport

The most popular entertainments are sports events, such as horse racing at Ellerslie Racecourse, or rugby football (in winter) at Eden Park. Internationally, the Anniversary Day Regatta (4th Monday in January) is billed as the world's greatest one-day regatta, with yachts and other boats of all sizes dotting the Waitemata Harbour and gulf.

An international standard motor racing Grand Prix is usually held in mid-January. There are tennis and golf tournaments in summer, and sports events of many kinds, between suburban teams, are held every Saturday.

Music and Theatre

The **Aotea Centre** and **Town**

Hall often feature orchestral concerts (the Auckland Philharmonia is the local orchestra) and visiting artists. Auckland is on the international circuit for famous musicians and shows. There are also a number of amateur theatrical groups in the greater Auckland area.

Nightlife

Auckland is not renowned for its nightlife – the normal pub closing time is 22.00hrs. There are a number of 'nightclubs' offering disco music. **Stanley's** in Queen Street is a recommended nightclub, while **No. 7** offers jazz Wednesday to Sunday nights.

The **Sheraton** and **Pan Pacific** hotels both have late night bar-cafés, while **Burgundys of Parnell** offers a cabaret revue. The **Shakespeare Tavern** (Albert and Wyndham Streets corner) attracts a mixed crowd with its beer brewed on the premises. Many of the suburban taverns have loud bands to drink by, amid varying standards of comfort.

There are some 'girlie' shows close to the foot of Queen Street, and also in Karangahape Road. There are a number of movie theatres, usually with recent releases, in the town centre and suburbs.

Shopping

Central Auckland is almost a one-street town for shopping, with Queen Street serving both city business people and tourists. However, Queen Street leads up the hill to Karangahape Road – a mixed and more cosmopolitan shopping area, near the Sheraton Hotel. Souvenirs on offer here include sheepskin rugs and Maori carvings. Central Auckland has only one large department store – **Smith and Caughey** in the main street, good for basic shopping. The **Downtown Mall** near the foot of Queen Street offers 'off-street' shopping. **Newmarket** and **St Lukes** both offer good suburban shopping within a few miles of the city centre. Trendy **Parnell** is an older area that has been revitalised and is full of shops, cafés and courtyards – very popular. The **Victoria Park Market**, a half-mile (1km) walk west of downtown, is popular with locals and tourists alike, selling souvenirs and fresh food. Open daily until 19.30 hours.

The **China Oriental Markets**, a couple of blocks east of the city centre, are a new variation on the market theme. Open daily until 18.00hrs.

Some think that general shopping standards in the city centre have deteriorated over recent years, as many citizens of this sprawling city now prefer to shop in suburban malls. For other shopping try heading north to Takapuna, east to Pakuranga, west to Lynmall, or south to Manukau City Centre.

Tourist Information: the Visitor Information Centre is at 299 Queen Street, next to Aotea Square (tel: (09) 366 6888); there is also a Visitor Information Centre at Auckland International Airport.

WHAT TO SEE IN THE NORTHERN REGION

◆◆◆
BAY OF ISLANDS ✓

About 150 miles (240km) by road north of Auckland, this is one of New Zealand's most historic regions, as well as being one of the North Island's most popular resort areas.
The **Bay of Islands Maritime and Historic Park** is an area of coastal beauty with more than 500 miles (800km) of indented coastline, 150 small islands, and many mainland reserves. The Bay is internationally known for sailing and is a base for big game fishing.
Paihia, Russell, and Waitangi are the three most important towns around the Bay. Kawakawa and Kerikeri are local servicing towns – the latter with an airport.

Russell
The town – then named Kororarcka was known in the early 1800s as 'the hell hole of the South Pacific', where lawless whalers and traders came into often violent contact with the native Maoris. After the signing of the 'Waitangi Treaty' between the British Government and the Maoris in 1840, Russell became the first capital of New Zealand – for a few months. Now it is a quiet settlement, almost a backwater, although it is the headquarters of the Maritime and Historic Park and centre for big game fishing.
There are also a number of historic sites and tourist attractions, including **Captain Cook Memorial and Russell Centennial Museum**, with displays on the town's history including a replica of Captain Cook's ship *Endeavour*.
Open: daily 10.00–16.00hrs.
The **Christ Church**, built in 1834, is New Zealand's oldest surviving church. It bears musket ball holes from a skirmish between the British navy and Maori 'rebels' in 1845,

North Island's Bay of Islands

THE NORTHERN REGION

and the churchyard contains graves of sailors killed. Nearby **Pompallier House** (1844) was part of the first Roman Catholic mission. Open: 10.00–16.30hrs. A short steep road leads up **Flagstaff Hill** (or Maiki Hill), where rebel leader Hone Heke three times cut down the flagpole, which carried the British flag.

Paihia
Most visitors to Bay of Islands make this their headquarters. It has a small shopping area and plenty of accommodation. The town spreads out over three bays, all suitable for summer swimming.
Paihia wharf is the departure point for ferries across to Russell, and for Bay cruises. A cruise around the Bay of at least half a day is highly recommended. The **Church of St Paul** stands on the site of New Zealand's first church, built in 1823; the present building dates from 1926. It was also here that, in 1834, New Zealand's first printing press printed the New Testament in Maori.
The **Musuem of Shipwrecks**, between Paihia and Waitangi, is a renovated barque on which are displayed marine relics and treasure retrieved from shipwrecks found around the New Zealand coast.
Open: daily 10.30–17.00hrs.

Waitangi
Just around the Bay a little north of Paihia, is Waitangi, largely a historic reserve. It contains a house built in 1834 for the 'British Resident' James Busby,

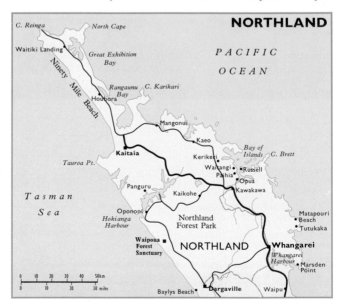

who drafted the Waitangi Treaty. It is now known as the Treaty House, because it was here that the controversial 1840 Treaty was signed. A copy of the Treaty, as well as other relics of the time, are housed here.

Open: daily 09.00–17.00hrs.

Close by is the **Maori Centennial Memorial Meeting House**, erected in 1940, with carved decoration. In a neighbouring building is a 121-foot (37m) carved Maori War canoe. A ceremony is held on Waitangi Day, 6 February, each year, to commemorate the signing of the Treaty, when the canoe is launched.

Kerikeri

Kerikeri, 14 miles (23km) from Paihia, is a picturesque and flourishing citrus fruit growing centre and arts and crafts community. Just past the commercial area is the site of New Zealand's second mission station. The **Kerikeri Mission House** (also known as Kemp House, after the mission family who lived there) was erected in 1821, and is the oldest surviving European building in the country.

Open: daily 10.00–12.30 and 13.30–16.30hrs.

Next door the old **Stone Store**, completed in 1835, still contains a shop and museum. Just over the bridge at Kerikeri Inlet is **Rewa's Village** – a reconstruction of a Maori village in pre-European times.

Excursions

From Paihia there are various Bay cruises available – including one in a full-sailed

Setting sail off the North Island

schooner. Day bus tours visit other parts of Northland – the most popular being the full day tour to Cape Reinga (see page 28). There are also day trips in summer to the Waipoua Kauri Forest (see page 36).

Accommodation

(Area code: 09). The top hotel in the area is the **Waitangi Resort Hotel**, Waitangi, Bay of Islands (tel: 402 7411), with pleasant grounds and extensive views. Paihia has more moderate hotel accommodation at **Autolodge**, Marsden Road, Paihia (tel: 402 7416), while motel accommodation is available at the **Abel Tasman Lodge**, Waterfront, Paihia (tel: 402 7521), and a number of others. Across the Bay big game fishermen frequent the old but

dignified **Duke of Marlborough**, The Strand (tel: 403 7829), at Russell.
For campers there is **Smiths Holiday Camp**, along the Paihia–Opua road, a mile (1.6km) from Paihia (with its own private bay) (tel: 402 7678).

Restaurants

Seafood features prominently in the local restaurants. At Paihia try **Esmae's** or **The Tides**, and in Russell **The Gables** restaurant, on the waterfront.

◆◆
CAPE REINGA

This is New Zealand's 'Land's End' – the northwestern tip of the North Island, where the Tasman Sea meets the Pacific Ocean. For the Maori people, it was the 'place of leaping', where the dead set off for their homeland across the sea. The views are magnificent. There is road access, but a one-day coach tour from Paihia, or the town of Kaitaia further north, is the easy way of doing the trip. Part of the return journey is along the 56 miles (90km) of so-called **Ninety Mile Beach** with its great sand dunes.
Cape Reinga has a lighthouse (not open to the public), but no commercial facilities. There are pleasant beaches and a basic camping ground on adjacent bays; also a shop and restaurant several kilometres back at Waitiki Landing.
On the way to the Cape make a stop at the **Wagener Museum** at Houhora to see a collection of natural history items and household and other bric-à-brac from the past.

Open: daily 08.00–17.00hrs. Please note that beach driving is not for the inexperienced, not permitted in rental vehicles, and that northern access to the beach is restricted to buses only.

◆
HAMILTON

80 miles (127km) south of Auckland
One of New Zealand's larger cities, Hamilton lies inland, astride the Waikato River – the country's longest waterway. The town was established in two sections, one on each river bank, as soldiers' settlements after the Waikato land wars of the 1860s. The surrounding Waikato region is a rich agricultural area. For four days each June the National Field Days, the southern hemisphere's largest showcase of agricultural and horticultural products, is held at the Mystery Creek showgrounds. Here too, is situated the **National Agricultural Heritage** theme park, which offers live animal shows, a timber display, and museums concerned with dairying and Clydesdales – you can see some of these great horses here.
Open: Thursday to Sunday 09.00–17.00hrs.
In the **Hamilton Gardens** are 143 acres (58 hectares) of greenhouse displays, a camellia garden, a rose garden and many other flowers and trees.
Open: daily. Admission free.
There are other parks for strolling or picnicking on the banks of the Waikato River, and also at Hamilton Lake, on the

west side of town. The MV
Waipa Delta offers paddleboat
cruises on the river.

Accommodation

Most Hamilton accommodation
is of the motel or motor inn
style, with a good range and
standard. Possibilities are:
Southern Cross Motor Inn,
Ulster Street (tel: (07) 838
3299), or the **Fountain City
Motor Inn**, 305 Ulster Street
(tel: (07) 839 3107).

Restaurants

For family eating try **Cobb &
Co** at the **Commercial
Establishment Hotel**, in
Victoria Street.
For more selective dining there
is **Seddon House** in Seddon
Street, **Anderson's** in London
Street, or **Montana Restaurant**
in Victoria Street. For fast food,
Kentucky Fried Chicken and
Pizza Hut are represented.

Shopping

Hamilton's main shopping
street is Victoria Street. Note
particularly the **Centrepoint
Mall** halfway along. There is a
suburban mall at Chartwell
Square.

Information: Hamilton Visitor
Centre, Anglesea Street (tel:
(07) 839 3360).

◆◆◆
ROTORUA ✓

*145 miles (234km) southeast of
Auckland*
The first thing you notice as you
approach Rotorua is a
pervading hydrogen sulphide
smell from the geothermal
activity. If the pleasures of hot
springs, geysers and boiling
mud begin to pall, the area also
has attractive lakes and both
indigenous and exotic forests.
Rotorua is also a centre for
Maori art and culture.
The town of Rotorua was
established in the late 19th
century, when the curative
waters of the thermal springs
were recognised by Europeans
as therapeutic (the Maoris had
long known about them). The
district's early growth was
hindered by the 1886 eruption
of Mount Tarawera, which
devastated three Maori
villages, killing 150 people, and
destroying the extraordinary
pink and white silica terraces
which had been a tourist
attraction. In 1895, trout were
released in the lakes, starting the
present large fishing activity.

*Cape Reinga, looking out to the
wide blue yonder*

Geothermal Sights

Rotorua's thermal activity is part of a band of volcanic activity that stretches through a large part of central North Island. The **Whakarewarewa Thermal Reserve**, commonly known as 'Whaka', features the popular geysers known as Pohutu and the Prince of Wales Feathers. Pohutu can spout every 30 minutes, spurting hot water to a height of up to 100 feet (30m), but is not predictable. There is a replica of a Maori village here, and examples of how the hot pools were used for bathing and cooking.

The entrance to Whaka is through the **New Zealand Maori Arts and Crafts Institute**, which helps preserve Maori traditions.

Open: daily 08.30–16.30hrs. Admission charge (except for Maori Arts and Crafts Institute which is free).

A lesser (but free) example of thermal activity is at **Kuirau Park**, on Ranolf Street, and also on some stretches of the shores of Lake Rotorua. At **Ohinemutu**, a small suburban village not far from the downtown area, some smaller steam vents bubble beside the Maori Anglican St Faith's Church, known for its carvings and modern etched window depicting Christ dressed in a Maori cloak of feathers.

Some 10 miles (16km) northeast, at **Tikitere**, there is a very active area with bubbling pools and boiling mud known as **Hell's Gate** (*open*: daily 09.00–17.00hrs), while to the south there are extensive geothermal areas at **Waimangu** (*open*: daily 08.30–17.00hrs) and **Waiotapu** (*open*: daily 08.30–17.00hrs).

These places all charge an admission fee.

When walking around any of Rotorua's thermal areas, stay on the paths as it can be dangerous to stray.

Other Sights

Launch cruises on **Lake Rotorua** are available from the bottom of the city's main street. Attractions of the region's ten major lakes include the bush drive to lake Okataina, the thermal activity around Lake Rotomahana, and the colours of the so called Blue and Green Lakes (Lakes Tikitapu and Rotokakahi). A popular full day trip, known as the **Waimangu Round Trip**, combines the Waimangu thermal valley with two lake trips, a short walk between the two lakes, and a

visit to the remains of the **Te Wairoa Maori Village** buried in the 1886 eruption (*open*: daily 08.30–17.00hrs).

Three or four major springs feed Lake Rotorua. They all feature trout pools for viewing. The closest to the city, and winner of a tourism award, is the combined **Rainbow and Fairy Springs**, in a natural bush environment (*open*: daily 08.00–17.00hrs). Adjacent is **Rainbow Farm** with animal displays (open same hours). Also nearby, the **Skyline Gondola** ride to a viewpoint (*open*: daily 09.00–16.30hrs). Situated five miles (8km) out at Ngongotaha, the **Agrodome** gives a popular display of sheep, dogs and shearing. *Show times*: 09.15, 11.00 and 14.30hrs daily. Entry charge. Town walks include **Rotorua**

Prince of Wales Feathers, Rotorua

Government Gardens (just a few blocks from the main shopping street), and **Redwood Memorial Grove** near Whaka. Within the grounds of the Government Gardens are the **Polynesian Pools**, hot thermal baths, both public and private, also offering massage and sauna facilities. *Open*: daily 09.00–22.00hrs. Back downtown in Hinemoa Street, there is a large landscaped flower display in the **Orchid Gardens**. *Open*: daily 08.30–17.30hrs. Admission charge.

Accommodation

Accommodation is plentiful and varied – mostly to a very satisfactory standard. (Area code: 07). Up-market travellers are well catered for at the **Sheraton** in Fenton Street (tel: 348 7139), or **Kingsgate**, in Eruera Street (tel: 347 1234). Motor inn style accommodation includes **Lake Plaza Rotora**, Eruera Street (tel: 348 1174), **Devonwood Manor**, 312 Fenton Street (tel: 348 1999), and **Regal Geyserland Hotel**, Fenton Street (tel: 348 2039). For motels consider **Wylie Court Motor Lodge**, 345 Fenton Street (tel: 347 7879) among many. Among the many campgrounds are **Rotorua Thermal Holiday Park** near Whakarewarewa Thermal Reserve (tel: 346 3140) and **Holdens Bay Holiday Park** (tel: 345 9925).

Restaurants

All of Rotorua's leading hotels regularly offer *hangi* style

Colourful traditional Maori dance can be seen at most of Rotorua's leading hotels

precinct – but shops also overflow on to neighbouring side streets. The village shops outside Whakarewarewa are a favourite centre for local arts and crafts.

Hillside Herbs at the bottom of the Skyline Gondola is another interesting souvenir shop, specialising in fragrant items (soaps, pot-pourri, etc) and plants.

Entertainment
All leading hotels feature an evening *hangi* dinner (food cooked in an earth oven), along with Maori traditional dancing and singing. Reservations are essential.

Other attractions are boating and fishing trips, and also aerial scenic flights over the surrounding district.

Information: Tourism Rotorua, 67 Fenton Street (tel: (07) 348 5179).

dinners with a Maori concert. Among the downtown restaurants try **Caesars** for New Zealand lamb or **Lewishams**, 115 Tutanekai Street, for continental cuisine. For family meals consider **Cobb & Co**, in Hinemoa Street. **Pizza Hut** and **McDonalds** are represented in the central district.

For dining with a view try **Aorangi Peak Restaurant** up Mount Ngongotaha (Mountain Road), or, the restaurant at the top of the Skyline Gondola.

Shopping
Rotorua's main shopping street is Tutanekai Street – part of which is a closed off parking

♦♦♦
TAUPO ✓

174 miles (280km) southeast of Auckland
Nestling on the side of New Zealand's largest lake, the popular holiday and fishing centre of Taupo lies at the very centre of the North Island. Lake Taupo has an area of 239 square miles (619sq km) at an altitude of 1,210 feet (369m) above sea-level. The lake is a water-filled volcanic crater, the result of huge explosions in the past, and there are pockets of thermal activity around it. The **Wairakei Geothermal Power Station**, five miles (9km) north

of Taupo, with its many pipes and belching steam, is a facility which harnesses geothermal activity to generate electricity at a nearby powerhouse. You may drive through the field (in daylight hours only) to the viewpoint at the far end. There is also a tourist information centre on the main road. Close by is the **Craters of the Moon** thermal area – a weird (and currently free) area of boiling cauldrons in a pine forest. Take care here, especially with children.

Nearby, at **Huka Falls** the Waikato river, Lake Taupo's outflow, cascades through a narrow chasm and falls over a 36-foot (11m) ledge. There is road and pedestrian access. Also near by is the **Aratiatia Rapids**. Here the Waikato River is diverted through a tunnel for hydro-electric power generation. However, at 10.00hrs and 14.30hrs daily, the water is diverted over the old riverbed. The river drops 92 feet (28m) in 3,025 feet (906m) and the spectacle of the dry rocky riverbed suddenly changing to a foaming torrent is dramatic.

Accommodation and Restaurants

(Area code: 07). Taupo has a big selection of good motels, including the **Cascades Motor Lodge**, (tel: 378 3774) and the **Oasis Beach Resort** (tel: 378 9339), both on Lake Terrace. More stylish motor inns include **Manuels**, Lake Terrace (tel: 378 5110).

At Wairakei the **Wairakei Hotel** (tel: 374 8021) offers

accommodation of a good standard, along with an international-class golf course, while the nearby exclusive **Huka Lodge**, Huka Falls Road, Taupo (tel: 378 5791), is an all-inclusive tourist resort and is expensive. There are several motorcamps.

Manuels Restaurant offers up-market eating, while there is a family style **Cobb & Co** restaurant at the reasonably priced **Lake Establishment Hotel**.

Shopping

Shops line one side of the main thoroughfare Tongariro Street, but there are more shops on the side streets adjoining this thoroughfare.

Information: Information Taupo, 13 Tongariro Street (tel: 378 9000).

◆◆
TAURANGA
128 miles (206km) southeast of Auckland

Tauranga, and its adjacent thriving port of Mount Maunganui, lie on the shore of the Bay of Plenty – so named by Captain Cook in 1769, after some favourable trading with native Maori tribes. The area is perhaps more of a retirement town than a tourist resort, but is often included on a three to four day excursion south from Auckland because of its historic interest.

Tauranga was a site of conflict between Maori tribes, and then, in the battle of Gate Pa, between British forces and the Maoris in 1864. **Tauranga Historic Village** in 17th Avenue

West is a living museum in the form of an early colonial village, with houses, shops, train, wharf and sawmill.
Open: daily 09.00–18.00hrs (16.00 in winter). Admission charge.
One of the country's leading ports, Mount Maunganui, commonly known as 'The Mount' is linked to Tauranga by toll bridge across the harbour. **Ocean Beach**, an eight-mile (13km) stretch of sandy beach, is the main attraction. **The Mount** itself is a 761-foot (232m) volcanic peak. At the foot of the Mount are unique hot salt water swimming pools. There are walks to the top and also around the base of the hill. Traces of old Maori *pa* (fortress) are visible.

Accommodation and Restaurants

(Area code: 07). The **Willow Park International**, 9 Willow Street (tel: 578 9119), is Tauranga's best hotel. The **Roselands Motel** (tel: 578 2294) and **Monmouth Park Motel** (tel: 578 0177) are both nearby. There are several motorcamps and holiday parks.
For dining, consider **Olivers Restaurant** in Devonport Road, **Charlie Browns** on Cameron Road, or the **Chart House** overlooking the marina.

Shopping

Devonport Road is Tauranga's main shopping street, but the adjacent streets also have many shops. There are more shops and a mall at Mount Maunganui.

Information: Tauranga Information and Visitors Centre, The Strand (tel: 578 8103).

◆◆
THAMES AND THE COROMANDEL PENINSULA

70 miles (115km) south of Auckland

The small town of Thames at the base of the Coromandel Peninsula is off the main tourist routes, but it is gateway to a peninsula of rugged beauty. The area's heyday was during the days of the gold rush in the late 1860s. Most Thames and Coromandel gold was from quartz rock, which required big stampers to crush it. There are still many traces of gold mines and old stamper batteries in the area. The town also has museums and other relics of those days.

Kauaeranga Valley

Seven miles southeast of Thames, this scenic and historic bush area once had an extensive timber milling

The Coromandel Peninsula

industry, centred particularly on the valuable kauri trees. There are now picnic sites and many bush walks.

Karangahake Gorge
To the south of Thames, the gorge is a short steep-sided valley between the small towns of Paeroa and Waihi. A 2½-mile (4.5km) walkway following a now closed railway (partly through a tunnel) shows gold mining remains and fine, scenic views.

Coromandel Peninsula
The peninsula, surrounded by scenic coastline and beach resorts is very popular with Aucklanders during the summer months. The peninsula itself is a rugged mountain range, and its dense forest covering gives a good idea of the type of vegetation which New Zealanders call 'bush'. Around the coast are plenty of empty beaches off the beaten track.

The small town of **Coromandel** is 33 miles (53km) up the west coast of the peninsula via a scenic route along the foreshore of the Firth of Thames. It has a mining museum and some good colonial architecture.

Whitianga is a summer resort and big game fishing town on the eastern side.

Accommodation
(Area code: 07). In Thames, **Brian Boru**, Pollen Street (tel: 868 6523), is a colonial style hotel (1868) with atmosphere and reasonable prices. For motel style there is the **Coastal Motor Lodge**, 608 Tauru Road (tel: 868 6843). If you are looking for a campground, go up the coast seven miles (11.5km) to the well-provided **Waiomu Bay Holiday Park** (tel: 868 2777).

Information: Thames Information Centre, 405 Queen Street (tel: 868 7284).

◆◆
TONGARIRO NATIONAL PARK
205 miles (331km) south of Auckland
The first of New Zealand's national parks was appointed in 1887, in the central North Island. It is known as the Tongariro National Park, but the tiny community adjacent is called National Park.

The park covers 185,000 acres (75,000 hectares) and is dominated by three volcanic peaks: Mounts Ruapehu (9,173

THE NORTHERN REGION

Tongariro's volcanic peaks

feet/2,796m); Ngauruhoe (7,513 feet/2,290m) and Tongariro (6,457 feet/1,968m). The first two are still active. Ruapehu has a warm crater lake surrounded by snow and ice; on Christmas Eve 1953, an eruption caused a torrent of water down the lake's river outlet to wash away a railway bridge minutes before a midnight express train tried to cross it – with 153 people killed. However, the mountains are usually placid.

Skiing
Ruapehu is the North Island's leading ski area – from late June to October.
Access to the mountain from the National Park settlement is via the **Whakapapa Village**, where accommodation, ski club huts, and the Park Headquarters (*open*: daily 08.00–17.00hrs) are located. The Top o' the Bruce Road climbs from here to 5,321 feet (1,622m) for ski-lifts and tows; mountain transport is provided during winter months. Access to the southern (Turoa) ski slopes is provided by the Mountain Road from Ohakune, 21 miles (35km) further south.

Walking
In summer the National Park is largely snow free, apart from the three peaks. The rocky, tussock-covered park has a number of walking tracks – from half-hour to five-day walks. Check into the Park Headquarters before taking any of the longer tracks, as mountain weather can change suddenly and dramatically. See also **Peace and Quiet**, page 93.

Accommodation
The **Grand Chateau** hotel, at Whakapapa Village (tel: (07) 892 3809), on the slopes of Mount Ruapehu is one of New Zealand's best known hotels. It has restaurants, indoor swimming pool, sauna, etc. Most of the other accommodation in the area is of more basic ski lodge variety.

◆
WAIPOUA FOREST SANCTUARY
155 miles (250km) north of Auckland
West of Paihia in the Bay of Islands is a stand of thick native bush known as the Waipoua Forest Sanctuary. It is retained as a forest park and contains the largest remnant of the extensive kauri forests which once covered much of the upper North Island. There are about 300 types of trees and plants found in this 22,200 acre (9,000 hectare) reserve. The kauri is a giant species of tree taking up to 1,000 years or more to mature. Kauris may grow to a height of 165 feet (50m) and a girth of 50 feet (15m). The tree was prized for ships' masts, and

for building, and its gum was also prized as a varnish. Now, however, the kauri is mostly protected, because of the devastation that occurred in the 19th century and the tree's very slow growth-rate.

The most famous tree in the Waipoua Forest is known as Tane Mahuta (meaning 'God of the Forest'). It is about 12 centuries old, and its first branch is 40 feet (12m) above the ground. The way to Tane Mahuta is marked from the roadside.

Most coach tours of the Northland area take in the forest. There are no commercial facilities.

◆◆◆
WAITOMO CAVES ✓

125 miles (202km) south of Auckland

Each of these famous limestone caves is noted for galleries, chambers, and stalactite and stalagmite formations, but the most popular of the three, **Waitomo Cave**, is especially renowned for its glow-worm grotto, where visitors glide on an underground stream gazing up at thousands of tiny lights on the roof. The New Zealand glow-worms are larvae of a small fly. There are tours hourly (more in the height of the summer season) through this cave between 09.00 and 16.30hrs.

The nearby **Aranui Cave** is rated the most beautiful (tours also available). There are many other caves in the area, and some are open for underground rafting and abseiling.

There is a hotel (**Waitomo Hotel**, tel: (07) 878 8227), but only a few other commercial facilities at Waitomo. The nearest towns are Otorohanga and Te Kuiti. Although Waitomo is not on the road from Auckland to Rotorua, many tour coaches deviate this way to include the cave.

◆
WHAKATANE

60 miles (96km) east of Tauranga

The town is on the Bay of Plenty, at the mouth of the Whakatane River, which forms its harbour. Its originated as a Maori stronghold. Now Whakatane lays claim to being the North Island's top sunshine town, and **Ohope Beach**, just 3½ miles (6km) further east over the headland, is a popular summer recreation area, offering surfing and fishing.

About 30 miles (50km) out in the Bay, opposite Whakatane, is White Island – an active volcano which belches steam, but fortunately little else. The island is a private reserve.

Accommodation and Restaurants

In Whakatane, try **Chatswood Manor**, a motel at 34 Domain Road (tel: (07) 307 0600). At Ohope Beach **West End Motels and Tourist Flats** are at 24 West End (tel: (07) 312 4665).

For eating, the **Chatswood Restaurant** or **The Reef Restaurant** are worth a try.

Information: Whakatane Information Office, Boon Street (tel: (07) 308 6058).

◆
WHANGAREI
105 miles (170km) north of Auckland

Whangarei, the main town north of Auckland, is a port, a commercial and industrial centre and a yachting base. An unusual attraction is the **Clapham Clock Museum** in the Central Park Rose Gardens. It has an interesting collection of more than 500 clocks and watches.
Open: daily 10.00–16.00hrs. Admission charge.
Northland Regional Museum is a historic house with exhibits in 60 acres (25 hectares) of grounds, three miles (5km) west of Whangarei.
Open: daily 10.00–16.00hrs. Admission charge.
On the northeastern edge of Whangarei town, at Tikipunga are **Whangarei Falls**, dropping 80 feet (24m) into a forest-surrounded pool.

Accommodation and Restaurants
(Area code: 09).
For overnighting in Whangarei, consider the **Settlers Hotel**, in Hatea Drive (tel: 438 2699); or the **Cherry Court Motor Lodge** 35 Otaika Road (tel: 438 3128). There are several motorcamps, including the **Tropicana Holiday Park** (tel: 436 0687) six miles (10km) out on the Whangarei Heads road.
For dining, try **The Myth**, the **Side Walk Café**, or **Bojangles Family Restaurant**.

Information: Whangarei Visitors Bureau, Tarewa Park, Otaika Road (tel: (09) 438 1079).

WELLINGTON AND CENTRAL NEW ZEALAND

Ancient bush, New Zealand's longest navigable river, quiet cattle-grazing country and hill sheep farms, together with the country's capital city, all go to make the pattern of the southern portion of the North Island.
There is history too. It was in the south of the East Cape region, near present-day Gisborne, where Captain Cook made the first European landing in New Zealand – to no welcome from the local Maoris. This easternmost part of the country is also noteworthy for being one of the first places on earth to see the sun rise every day.
On the west side of North Island is the homely, fertile agricultural and dairying region of Taranaki, based on the town of New Plymouth – known as 'The Garden City'.
Less gentle is the towering

Wellington's harbour and lights

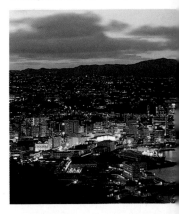

peak of Mount Egmont (or Taranaki as the Maoris call it), the dormant volcano which watches over New Plymouth and dominates wild Egmont National Park, with its varied bush terrain. Another National Park – designated only in 1987 – is Whanganui National Park, based on the great Whanganui River.

The river was once an important Maori canoe route and their villages lined its banks – remains of them can still be seen. According to Maori legend, the river's course was formed by Mount Taranaki as he fled from a successful rival in love.

The hilly country of the south and east is sheep country, and the town of Masterton sees one of the great sheep-shearing events of the Antipodes every March – the 'Golden Shears' competition.

Not least of the attractions of central New Zealand is Wellington, in its spectacular hilly setting on Port Nicholson harbour.

WELLINGTON

European settlement here began in 1840 after the land was bought from the Maori owners. Wellington became the capital of New Zealand in 1865, making it the seat of parliament and headquarters for government departments. An important commercial centre, it has excellent transport links with the rest of the country – by ferry, air, rail and coach.

The harbour is a focal point. Its beaches are popular with sunbathers and joggers, and sailors and windsurfers take advantage of its wide expanse. The central area of the city is compact, with shops, cafés and other facilities all within easy walking distance of each other. And to provide relief from the bustle of the city, there are plenty of gardens, parks and hilly view points.

Wellington has a reputation, at least partly justified, for being windy. The weather is certainly variable, and you should be prepared for almost anything.

WHAT TO SEE

◆◆
CABLE CAR
From midway along Lambton Quay, Wellington's main shopping street, a funicular type cable tram rises 400 feet (120m) over 1,970 feet (600m) up a 1-in-5 gradient at ten-minute intervals, to give views over the city and harbour. *Operates*: weekdays 07.00–22.00hrs; weekends 10.30–18.00hrs.

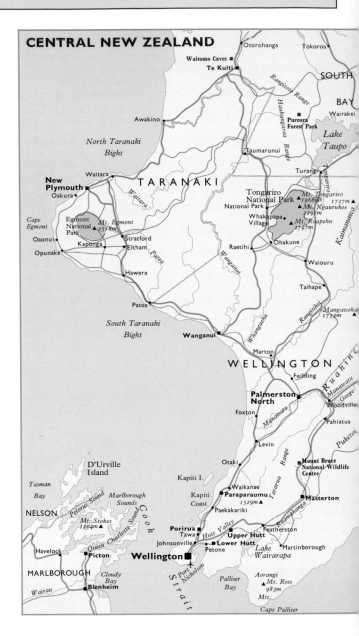

CENTRAL NEW ZEALAND

Otorohanga

Tokoroa

Waitomo Caves

Te Kuiti

SOUTH

BAY

Wairakei

Awakino

Pureora Forest Park

Rangitoto Range

Hauhungaroa Range

Lake Taupo

North Taranaki Bight

Waitara

New Plymouth

Oakura

T A R A N A K I

Waitara

Taumarunui

Turangi

Tongariro National Park

National Park

Cape Egmont

Egmont National Park

▲ Mt. Egmont 2518m

Stratford

Eltham

Whakapapa Village

▲ Mt. Tongariro 1968m 1727m
▲ Mt. Ngauruhoe 2291m
▲ Mt. Ruapehu 2797m

Oaonui

Kaponga

Patea

Ohakune

Raetihi

Kaimanawa

Opunake

Hawera

Wanganui

Waiouru

Patea

South Taranaki Bight

Wanganui

Whangaehu

Taihape

▲ *Mangaweka 1733m*

Marton

W E L L I N G T O N

Ruahine

Feilding

Palmerston North

Manawatu Gorge

Woodville

Foxton

Manawatu

Pahiatua

Puketoi

Levin

D'Urville Island

Tasman Bay

Marlborough Sounds

NELSON

Kapiti I.

Kapiti Coast

Otaki

Tararua Range

Mount Bruce National Wildlife Centre

Ruamahanga

Waikanae

Paraparaumu 1529m ▲

Masterton

Pelorus Sound

▲ *Mt. Stokes 1204m*

Queen Charlotte Sound

C o o k

Paekakariki

Porirua

Tawa

Featherston

Martinborough

Havelock

Picton

Johnsonville

Hutt Valley

Upper Hutt

Lower Hutt

Petone

Lake Wairarapa

Wellington

MARLBOROUGH

Cloudy Bay

Blenheim

Wairau

S t r a i t

Port Nicholson

Palliser Bay

Aorangi ▲ *Mt. Ross 983m Mts.*

Cape Palliser

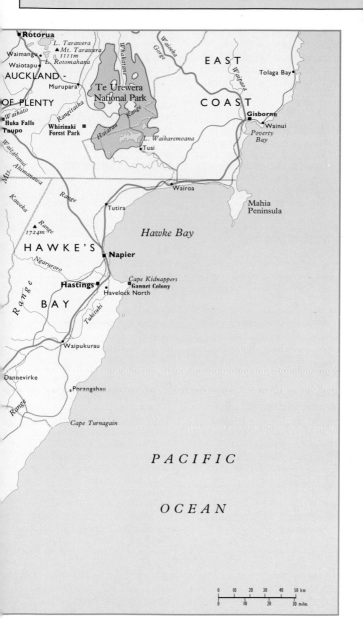

Rotorua
L. Tarawera
▲ Mt. Tarawera
1111m
Waimangu
Waiotapu · L. Rotomahana
AUCKLAND -
Murupara
OF PLENTY
Waikato
Huka Falls
Taupo
Waitahanui
Ahimanawa

Te Urewera
National Park
Whirinaki
Forest Park
Rangitaiki
Whakatane
Huiarau Range

Waioeka
Gorge
Waipaoa

EAST

Tolaga Bay

COAST

Gisborne
Wainui
Poverty
Bay

L. Waikaremoana
Tuai

Mts.

Kaweka

Range

Range
1724m

Wairoa

Tutira

Mahia
Peninsula

Hawke Bay

HAWKE'S

Ngaruroro

Napier

Range

BAY

Hastings
Havelock North
Tukituki

Cape Kidnappers
Gannet Colony

Waipukurau

Dannevirke

Porangahau

Range

Cape Turnagain

PACIFIC

OCEAN

0   10   20   30   40   50 km

0   10   20   30 miles

At the top is an entrance to the **Botanic Gardens**. A walk downhill through these gardens, which include formal and wild areas, is an alternative to riding back on the cable car.

◆

MARINE DRIVE
This is a signposted 19-mile (30km) route from Oriental Bay, around the Miramar peninsula, taking in the harbour and its entrance. There are fine views of bays and beaches.

◆

MARITIME MUSEUM
Jervois Quay
The Wellington Harbour Board houses a nautical display in their 'Shed 11' building on the quay. The museum features models, pictures and relics particularly related to Wellington maritime history.
Open: Monday to Friday 09.30–16.00hrs; reduced hours at weekends.

◆◆◆

MOUNT VICTORIA
The windy 643-foot (196m) peak of Mount Victoria offers an expansive panorama of Wellington city and harbour. The route to the top is signposted.

◆◆

MUSEUM OF NEW ZEALAND
Buckle Street
The Museum of New Zealand complex is about one and a half miles (2km) from the central downtown area. It houses displays on Maoris, Polynesians, and early settlers. There are also geology,

palaeontology and botany sections dating back to the 1860s; and some relics of Captain Cook's voyages.
Open: daily 09.00–17.00hrs.
Adjacent are the **National Art Gallery, Shrine of Remembrance**, and **National War Memorial**.

◆

NATIONAL ARCHIVES
10 Mulgrave Street, Thorndon
Documents here include the original Treaty of Waitangi.
Open: Monday to Friday 09.00–17.00hrs.

◆◆

NATIONAL LIBRARY OF NEW ZEALAND
Molesworth Street
Contains historic collections and manuscripts including the famous Alexander Turnbull Library.
Open: Monday to Friday 09.00–17.00hrs.

◆◆

PARLIAMENT BUILDINGS
Bowen Street
The Parliament Building (built 1922) contains the House of Representatives. A small entrance beside the main steps is the office for visitor tours on weekdays (consult the City Information Centre for times or tel: (04) 471 9457). It is not permitted to wander around unescorted. Adjacent is the '**Beehive**', a round building designed by British architect Sir Basil Spence and erected in 1981. It houses ministerial offices and the Cabinet room. Close by is the Gothic-style **General Assembly Library**,

Old and new meet at Parliament

built in 1897; and **Old St Paul's**, a church built in 1866 from native timbers in a Gothic revival style. Also near by is the 1876 **Government Building**, the largest wooden building in the southern hemisphere.

Suburbs

◆
HUTT VALLEY
The Hutt Valley, to the north, with the suburbs of Petone, Lower Hutt and Upper Hutt is part of Wellington metropolitan area. It is a flat expanse, built up with housing and industry. Up that way, look for the **Petone Settlers Museum** displaying local history and culture.
Open: Monday to Friday 10.00–16.00hrs; weekends 11.00–17.00hrs.
Dowse Art Museum, in Lower Hutt, displays local and touring art exhibitions.
Open: Tuesday to Friday 12.00–16.00hrs; weekends 13.00–17.00hrs.

◆◆
KAPITI COAST
The Kapiti Coast consists of the dormitory suburbs of Porirua, Paekakariki and Paraparaumu. These outer suburbs feature a number of specialist museums including a steam train museum and a tram museum at Paekakariki. Notable at Paraparaumu is the **Southward Car Museum**, a fine and famous collection of veteran and vintage cars.
Open: daily 09.00–16.30hrs.

Accommodation
(Area code: 04).
The following offer up-market accommodation:
James Cook Centra, The Terrace, downtown (tel: 499 9500). 260 rooms, first class.
Plaza International, Wakefield Street, central (tel: 473 3900). 183 rooms, first class.
Quality Inn Plimmer Towers, corner of Boulcott Street and Gilmer Terrace, central (tel: 473 3750). 93 rooms, first class.

Less expensive but of a good standard are:

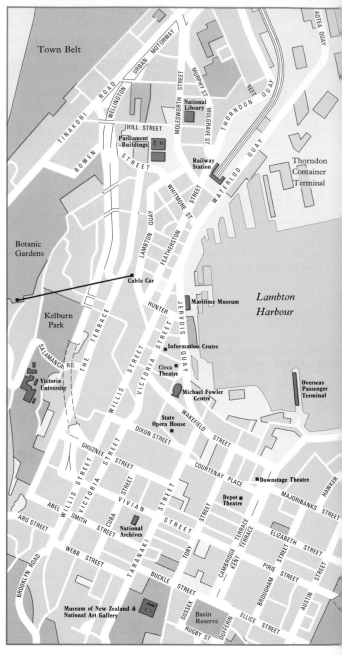

WELLINGTON

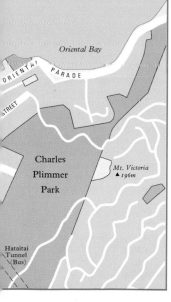

*Port Nicholson
(Wellington Harbour)*

Oriental Bay

ORIENTAL PARADE

STREET

Charles
Plimmer
Park

Mt. Victoria
▲ 196m

Hataitai
Tunnel
(Bus)

Academy Motor Lodge, 327 Adelaide Road (tel: 389 6166), one mile (1.6km) out. 16 rooms, self-contained motel units.

Bay Plaza, 40 Oriental Parade, central (tel: 385 7799). 78 rooms.

Hotel Raffaele, 360 Oriental Parade, one mile (1.6km) out (tel: 384 3450). 60 rooms with views.

St George Hotel, Willis Street, downtown (tel: 473 9139). 91 rooms, older hotel but good standard.

Sharella Motor Inn, 20 Glenmore Street, half a mile (1km) out (tel: 472 3823). 66 rooms, opposite gardens. Flag chain.

Wellington Parkroyal, Featherston Street, central (tel: 472 2722). New, first class.

For budget accommodation try:
Rowena City Lodge, 115 Brougham Street, Mount Victoria (tel: 385 7872). 50 rooms, budget bed and breakfast.

Terrace Travel Lodge, 291 The Terrace, near downtown (tel: 382 9506). 11 rooms.

Trekkers Hotel, Cuba Street, central (tel: 385 2153). 101 rooms; moderate standard.

In the suburbs are:
Abbey Court Motel, 7 Pharazyn Street, Lower Hutt, north harbour suburb (tel: 569 3967). 19 units, some with cooking facilities.

Foreshore Motor Lodge, corner of Esplanade and Nelson Streets, Petone, north harbour suburb (tel: 568 3609). 15 units, some with cooking facilities.

Hawks Inn Motel, 704 Fergusson Drive, Upper Hutt,

north harbour suburb (tel: 528 0130). 10 units, motel style.

There are also campgrounds in the Hutt Valley (north harbour) and Kapiti Coast (north coast) areas.

Restaurants
Most of the hotels listed have restaurants. Other restaurants include:

Bellissimo, Dukes Arcade; corner of Manners and Willis Streets, downtown; Italian style.

Bombay Bicycle, 228 Main Street, Upper Hutt (19 miles/30km from Wellington City); 'art style food'; located out in the suburbs.

Dockside Restaurant, seafood in refurbished Shed 3, Queens Wharf, Jervois Quay, downtown.

Fisherman's Table, Main Road, Paekakariki (approximately 25 miles/40km from Wellington city); seafood and sea views.

Il Casino, 108 Tory Street, central; top Italian.

Marbles, 87 Upland Road, Kelburn, inner suburb; New Zealand cuisine.

Petit Lyon, Courtenay Place; leading a la carte service.

Quayside, 245 Oriental Parade, Oriental Bay; brasserie.

Rose & Crown, BNZ Centre, corner of Willis Street and Lambton Quay; upmarket bistro.

Tinakori Bistro, 328 Tinakori Road, Thorndon; small and busy with New Zealand cuisine.

Tug Boat on the Bay, Oriental Bay; restaurant in a unique setting on a moored tugboat.

Turners, barbecue and grill, offers steaks and salads in Willis Street, downtown.

Wellington Settlement, 155 Willis Street, central; New Zealand food, piano, BYO.

Entertainment and Nightlife
While 'rugby, racing and beer' have been purported to sum up New Zealand's culture, the capital tries hard to present a softer image, although it is not evident in the annual Nissan Mobil 500 saloon car race through city streets each December. That event has become an off-track carnival as well, with concerts and other entertainment.

Wellington's biennial Festival of the Arts (held in even years, in March) has become the premier event of its kind in New Zealand, with events including orchestral concerts, opera, ballet, modern dance and painting, as well as a 'Fringe' with all kinds of street performances.

The city is home for the New Zealand Symphony Orchestra, the Royal New Zealand Ballet Company and the Wellington City Opera.

The **Downstage Theatre**, corner of Cambridge Terrace and Courtenay Place, is usually considered Wellington's leading live theatre, presenting a varied repertoire ranging from Shakespeare to Noel Coward. **Circa Theatre**, Harris Street and the **Depot** in Alpha Street are two other theatres offering regular live performances. Nightclubs include **James Cabaret** in Hania Street; and **Alfies Cabaret** near Cuba Mall.

Shopping
Downtown Wellington has a

reasonably big and vital shopping area.

Curving Lambton Quay is the leading street, but Willis Street and Manners Street are also shopping thoroughfares – the three string out in one long line. There is an underground shopping centre near the intersection of Lambton Quay with Willis Street; and part of Cuba Street has been made into a pedestrian mall. There are boutiques and speciality shops in the modern arcades.

Kirkcaldie & Stains in Lambton Quay is one of the leading department stores.

For books, there are **Whitcoulls** and **Bennetts Bookshop** for government publications. Not just official publications, but books on a host of other subjects as well. There are also galleries displaying and selling contemporary paintings and other crafts.

The **Wakefield Market** in central Wellington is open at weekends.

For suburban shopping there is the **Queensgate Mall** in Lower Hutt and the **Maidstone Mall** in Upper Hutt. At Petone on weekends the **Settlers Market** is good for food and souvenirs. Heading out to the Kapiti Coast, there is a shopping centre at Porirua (the **K Mary Mall**), and the **Coastlands** shopping mall at Paraparaumu.

Information: Wellington City Information Centre is on the corner of Wakefield and Victoria Streets (Old Town Hall) (tel: (04) 801 4000). The AA Centre is at 342–352 Lambton Quay (tel: (04) 473 8738).

WHAT TO SEE IN CENTRAL NEW ZEALAND

◆

GISBORNE
340 miles (550km) northeast of Wellington

This was the first part of New Zealand to be discovered by Captain Cook in 1769. On Kaiti Beach he took possession of the country in the name of King George III of England, but after a confrontation with local Maoris, sailed away empty-handed, naming the locality Poverty Bay.

Today the flat land adjacent to the Bay is agriculturally rich – particularly for corn and grapes: the area is surrounded by sheep farms on hard-won hill land.

The town, on three rivers, has riverside walks, **Botanic Gardens** and museums, including **Gisborne Museum** with displays on Captain Cook and early settlers as well as a

Wellington's famous cable car

collection of Maori artefacts. *Museum open*: Monday to Friday 10.00–16.00hrs; reduced hours at weekends.

At **Kaiti Beach** is an obelisk marking Cook's first New Zealand landing. A statue of Cook tops **Kaiti Hill**, a good viewpoint over the city and immediate Poverty Bay area. The town beach, **Waikanae**, features a playground and marine drive. Further north is a succession of surf beaches, including popular **Wainui** three miles (5km) out on the scenic East Cape route. **Eastwoodhill Arboretum**, 22 miles (35km) out from Gisborne going northwest, contains 160 acres (65 hectares) of trees and flowers comprising the largest collection of northern hemisphere vegetation in New Zealand (*open*: daily).

Accommodation and Restaurants

The **Sandown Park Motor Inn**, Childers Road (tel: (06) 867 9299), offers a good standard of hotel accommodation, while **Orange Grove**, 540 Childers Road (tel: (06) 867 9978), and **Teal Motor Lodge**, 479 Gladstone Road (tel: (06) 868 4019), are good motel accommodation. There is a municipal motorcamp at Grey Street, Waikanae Beach. You can eat at the **China Palace Restaurant**, **L'Escalier** or **McDonalds**.

Information: Eastland and Gisborn District Information Centre, 209 Grey Street (tel: (06) 868 6139).

HASTINGS see NAPIER AND HASTINGS

◆
MASTERTON
63 miles (101km) northeast of Wellington

Masterton is the leading commercial centre for the agricultural area known as the Wairarapa, and a good hiking

Fun at Masterton's swimming pool

base for the Tararua Mountains. The hills of Wairarapa and the east coast are sheep-rearing areas, and in the first week of March, Masterton hosts the **Golden Shears** sheep shearing competition, an international event in the sheep world.

Queen Elizabeth Park, situated on the western bank of the Waipoua River, is a pleasant place to relax, with gardens, sports fields, play areas, a deer park and a miniature railway all to hand.

About 19 miles (30km) further north is the **Mount Bruce National Wildlife Centre**. A popular visitor attraction, with birds, such as kiwis and takahes and other animals, such as native bats, on display, it is also a centre for studying and breeding rare and endangered species.

Open: daily. Admission charge.

Accommodation

The **Solway Park Resort**, High Street (tel: (06) 377 5129), and the **Masterton Motor Lodge**, 250 High Street (tel: (06) 378 2585), both offer good standard accommodation. Campers should head for **Mawley Park** (tel: (06) 378 6454).

Information: Tourism Wairarapa Visitor Information Centre, 5 Dixon Street (tel: (06) 378 7373).

◆◆
NAPIER AND HASTINGS
about 195 miles (314km)
northeast of Wellington
These twin cities just 16 miles (26km) apart, are the main towns of Hawke's Bay region. Napier is a coastal city and port,

while Hastings is inland, the centre of an agricultural and wine-growing district.

Napier's main claim to fame is as an Art Deco city, and this came about through disaster. On 3 February 1931, a violent 2½-minute earthquake, followed by fires, killed 256 people and devastated the town. A feature of the earthquake was the upheaval of part of the harbour bed to form 10,000 acres (4,000 hectares) of new land.

Suburban housing and the area's airport now stand on this new land, but the downtown part of the city was rebuilt in the 'modern' Art Deco style so popular in the 1930s.

Napier's **Marine Parade** is an attractive foreshore separating city and surf. It has gardens, fountains, an aquarium, marineland and other amenities. These facilities are within walking distance of the central shopping streets. Nearby **Bluff Hill** provides an overlook of city and port.

There are botanical gardens on the slopes of Hospital Hill, and rose gardens in suburban Kennedy Park. There are two museums commemorating the earthquake, one of which features a simulated earthquake.

Hastings's **Windsor Park** has a well planned children's playground called **Fantasyland**. There are a number of parks with garden displays, while its adjacent borough of **Havelock North** is known for its private residential gardens. Beyond Havelock North rises **Te Mata Peak** (1,309 feet/399m), with extensive views.

Accommodation and Restaurants

For accommodation in Napier consider the **McLean Park Lodge Motel**, in a quiet, central location at 177 Wellesley Road (tel: (06) 835 4422), or the rather sombre but comfortable **Masonic Establishment**, on the corner of Marine Parade and Tennyson Street (tel: (06) 835 8689). **Kennedy Park**, at Storkey Street, Marewa (tel: (06) 843 9126), is Napier's leading campground for tourist flats, cabins and campsites.

For eating in Napier consider the **Courtyard Café** for light snacks, **Cobb & Co** for families and **Beaches Restaurant** for seafood with views. In Hastings try **Grannys** or **McGintys**.

Shopping

In Napier the main shopping streets downtown are Dickens and Emerson Streets, leading to Clive Square. Heretaunga Street is the place to shop in Hastings.

Information: Napier Visitor Information Centre, Marine Parade (tel: (06) 835 7579); Hastings Visitor Information Centre, Russell Street (tel: (06) 876 0205).

◆◆
NEW PLYMOUTH

220 miles (355km) northwest of Wellington

New Plymouth is situated on the North Island's west coast bulge. The surrounding area, called Taranaki, is dominated by the dormant 8,261-foot (2,518m) volcano, Mount Egmont (also known by the Maori name Mount Taranaki), also visible from parts of the city. The surrounding lands form one of New Zealand's most productive dairying districts, and offshore oil and gas have brought wealth.

New Plymouth is known for its parks and gardens (it is sometimes dubbed the Garden City), including **Pukekura Park** with two lakes, a begonia house and fernery; **Brooklands Park** with its natural amphitheatre bowl used for performances; and **Lake Mangamahoe Domain**, six miles (10km) south. A famous park, 18 miles (29km) out of town, is operated by the **Pukeiti Rhododendron Trust**. Featuring rhododendrons and azaleas in a native bush setting, it is best visited in September through November.

Open: daily 09.00–17.00hrs. Road access up the slopes of **Mount Egmont** is available from the inland side, to about 3,000

Under the volcano: farmstead at the foot of Mount Egmont

feet (900m), at three different places, for views and walks – walkers should not go alone, however, because of sudden weather changes. There is skiing on the mountain in winter. The road up North Egmont goes to North Egmont Visitors Centre. The road to East Egmont gives access to views and skiing. The third, on the southern side, leads through fine scenery to Dawson Falls. You can get food and lodgings on the last two routes.

The **Motunui** synthetic petrol plant (about 12 miles/20km east of New Plymouth) is the world's first commercial synthetic fuel plant, designed and built at a time when oil prices were rising. The plant is not open to visitors, but there is a tourist centre with a large model of the installation.

Accommodation and Restaurants

Hotels in New Plymouth include

the **Plymouth**, on the corner of Leach and Hobson Streets (tel: (06) 758 0589), and **The Devon** 390 Devon Street (tel: (06) 759 9099). **Northgate Manor** (tel: (06) 758 5324) and **Amber Court** (tel: (06) 758 0922), are motels. Cabins and campsites are available at **Princes Tourist Court**, 29 Princes Street, Fitzroy (tel: (06) 758 2566). For eating try the **Devon Seafood Smorgasbord** at The Devon, or **Gareths Restaurant**.

Shopping

Shopping is mainly in Devon Street (partially closed to traffic) and at nearby City Centre mall.

Information: New Plymouth Information Centre, corner of Liardet and Leach Streets (tel: (06) 758 6086) .

◆
PALMERSTON NORTH
90 miles (145km) north of Wellington

This is an inland city on the Manawatu River, the centre of a rich agricultural district. Massey University was founded as an agricultural college. The centre of the city is **The Square**, containing 17 acres (7 hectares) of gardens. **The Esplanade** by the river has rose gardens and sports grounds.

Rugby football enthusiasts should take in the **National Rugby Museum** on Cuba Street.
Open: 10.00–12.00 and 13.40–16.00hrs (Sunday 13.30–16.00hrs only).

The **Manawatu Gorge** starts 10 miles (16km) east of the city and winds through mountains.

Accommodation and Restaurants

The **Sherwood Motor Inn**, 250 Featherstone Street (tel: (06) 357 0909), and the **Coachman**, 134 Fitzherbert Avenue (tel: (06) 356 5065), are two possible places to stay. For campers there is the **Palmerston North Holiday Park** (tel: (06) 358 0349) a mile (1.6km) out of town, which also has tourist flats. For family eating consider **Cobb & Co**. Alternatives are **Palmerston's** and **Lusitania** restaurants.

Information: Palmerston North Information Centre, The Square (tel: (06) 358 5003).

◆
WANGANUI

121 miles (195km) north of Wellington

Wanganui is situated on the North Island's west coast, at the mount of New Zealand's longest navigable river, the Whanganui (with an 'h').

Queen's Park in the centre of Wanganui contains the War Memorial Hall, the **Sarjeant Art Gallery**, and the **Regional Museum**. The latter houses one of the country's finest collections of Maori artefacts, including a huge war canoe. *Open*: weekdays, 10.00– 16.30hrs; weekends, reduced hours. Admission charge. Across the City Bridge is a pedestrian tunnel leading to an elevator that rises 216 feet (66m) through a hill to the **Durie Hill Memorial Tower** (*lift*: daily 07.30–11.00hrs and 11.30–18.30hrs; charge). At the southern end of the Cobham Bridge, **St Pauls Memorial Church** at Putiki features ornate Maori carvings and decorations inside.

About a mile (1.6km) north of the city, **Virginia Lake** is a neatly laid out area of gardens, hot houses, lake and floating fountain. The ocean beach of **Castlecliff**, is five miles (8km) west of the city, where the river meets the sea.

The Whanganui River

The river which bisects the city was known as 'the Rhine of New Zealand' back in the days of crinoline skirts and paddle steamers. The Whanganui River remains a beautiful waterway through a rugged and remote part of the North Island. There was once a large Maori population along the river banks. The Whanganui National Park lies around parts of the river. Jet boat trips are available along most parts of the river. Near Wanganui there are afternoon cruises a little way up river to a winery for wine-tasting.

Accommodation and Restaurants

For accommodation, the **Avenue Motor Inn**, 379 Victoria Avenue (tel: (06) 345 0907), or the **Wanganui Motor Lodge** 14 Alma Road, Gonville (1 mile/1.6km from Wanganui) (tel: (06) 345 4742) might fit the bill.

You could also eat in either hotel, or try **Cables** or **Cameron House**.

Information: Wanganui Information Centre, 101 Guyton Street (tel: (06) 345 3286).

SOUTH ISLAND: CHRISTCHURCH AND THE NORTH

The northern part of New Zealand's South Island is a land of mountains, with scenic passes crossing the ranges of the Southern Alps from east to west – Arthur's Pass, Haast Pass and Lewis Pass. A popular rail route, the Tranz-Alpine Express, is a hassle-free way of enjoying the scenery.

The most spectacular natural attraction of this part of New Zealand must be the great Fox and Franz Josef Glaciers, which descend from snowfields 10,000 feet (3,000m) high to a region of rainforest just behind the west coast, a mere 1,000 feet (300m) above sea-level. The hardy can venture on to the ice, others may prefer a bird's-eye view from a plane or helicopter.

The glaciers are the main feature of Westland National Park. This park is only one of several in the northern half of the South Island, offering huge tracts of wild country for hikers and naturalists. There is the bush and beach scenery of Abel Tasman Park around Tasman Bay; the lakes and mountains of Nelson Lakes National Park in the northeast; or the limestone grotesqueries of Paparoa National Park on the west coast.

Discoveries of gold in the west brought hordes of wealth-seekers and led to the growth of towns such as Greymouth, Hokitika and Westport. The gold ran out, but the days of the gold rush are remembered through museums, reconstructed

Sheep shearing in South Island

settlements and old workings. For a contrast with the wild colonial life, there is no better New Zealand city than Christchurch, home from home for English visitors, with its parks and gardens and fine old buildings.

CHRISTCHURCH

Christchurch is the international gateway to the South Island, and its largest city, as well as capital of Canterbury province. Considered the most 'English' of New Zealand's cities, Christchurch is situated on the Canterbury Plains. Its port is to the east, at Lyttelton on Banks Peninsula, and old volcanic crater. It was here, in 1850, that

THE NORTH OF SOUTH ISLAND

Punting on the Avon

the first four ships of the 'Canterbury Association' arrived with settlers intending to develop a Church of England colony similar to the Church of Scotland settlement already established further south in Dunedin (see page 69).
The city is named after the Oxford University college where John Godley, the city's founding father, was educated. Christchurch's English origins are reflected in the trees that fill the city, in the Gothic architecture; and in the famous Christ's College, a private school in the mould of the English public school.
Christchurch is known as New Zealand's 'Garden City', with a third of its area taken up by green spaces.

WHAT TO SEE

◆
ARTS CENTRE
Worcester Street West
Housed in buildings which were once the home of Canterbury University, this complex is now a focal point for artists, craftspeople, musicians and performers. There is always something to see – and a market at weekends.
Open: generally 10.00–16.00hrs.

◆
AVON RIVER
This is an attractive stream meandering through the city. A riverside walk begins at the west end of Oxford Terrace and follows the Avon to Kilmore Street. On the river banks is **Hagley Park**, nearly 450 acres (180 hectares) of gardens, trees and sports fields. Adjacent are the **Botanic Gardens**, featuring a conservatory, rose garden and a display of ferns and alpine plants, and the **Millbrook Reserve** which contains gardens of azaleas and rhododendrons.

◆◆
CANTERBURY MUSEUM
Rolleston Avenue
This museum includes special displays on greenstone (New Zealand jade); a reconstruction of a pioneer street; and bones of the moa (New Zealand 's large extinct flightless bird). The fine Hall of Antarctic Discovery concentrates especially on the explorer Scott, who visited Christchurch

on his Antarctic expeditions. The Antarctic connection continues with Christchurch acting as supply and servicing base for the US programme, Operation Deep Freeze. Next door is the **Robert McDougall Art Gallery**, with its own permanent collection of local and overseas exhibits.
Open: daily 09.00 (Art Gallery 10.00 in winter) to 16.30hrs; to 18.00hrs in summer. Free.

◆◆
FERRYMEAD HISTORIC PARK
Bridle Path Road, Heathcote
A working transport and technology museum and pioneer village on the site of New Zealand's first railway in 1863 with trams, trains and fire engines.
Open: daily 10.00–16.30hrs. Admission charge.

◆
MONA VALE
Fendalton Road
A 1905 homestead with exotic trees and flowers.
Open: daily 08.00–17.30hrs (19.30 summer). Free.

◆◆◆
MOUNT CAVENDISH GONDOLA ✓

An aerial cable-car ride up the Port Hills to over-look Christchurch and its port of Lyttelton. Also a 'Time Tunnel' historical display at the top.
Open: daily 10.00–23.00hrs. Admission charge.

◆
ORANA WILDLIFE PARK
McLeans Island Road
This open-range wildlife reserve has displays of wildlife from New Zealand and around the world.
Open: daily 10.00–17.30hrs. Admission charge.

◆
THE SQUARE
The pedestrian area dominated

Christchurch cathedral and square

by its Gothic-type cathedral is
the city centre. A spiral
staircase leads up 147 feet
(45m) to a viewpoint atop the
cathedral.
 A popular attraction in the
Square is Christchurch's
'wizard', a colourful soapbox
orator who provides
provocative and stimulating
discussions most weekday
lunchtimes (except during June
and July).

Out of Town

◆◆
BANKS PENINSULA
To the southeast of
Christchurch, this is a large
volcanic outcrop with two
extinct craters, one of which
now forms Lyttelton Harbour,
and the other Akaroa Harbour.
The road up and over the Port
Hills which separate the
peninsula from the city, via

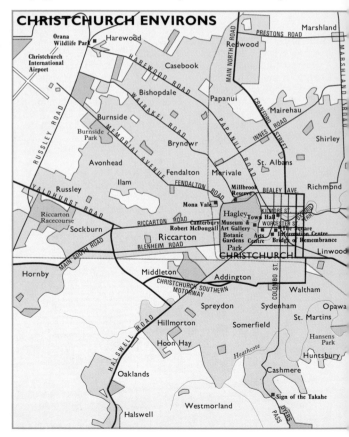

Dyer's Pass and the historic building known as the 'Sign of the Takahe' (now a restaurant) gives great views over city and harbour.

Akaroa 51 miles (82km) out of Christchurch was colonised by French settlers in 1840 just after Britain had declared its rule over New Zealand. It still has a French flavour and is a fascinating holiday area, on its pleasant harbour.

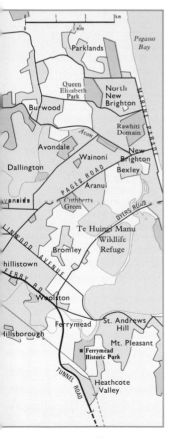

Beaches

Close to town are **New Brighton** (five miles/8km east) and **Sumner** (seven miles/11km southeast) beaches among others. Lyttelton Harbour is further afield, but has some beautiful secluded coves.

Other possible day trips include Hanmer Springs thermal resort, 85 miles (136km) or a ride on the spectacular Tranz-Alpine Express train via Arthur's Pass to Greymouth (see page 60). In winter it is also possible to make day trips to ski fields. Enquire locally regarding services and access.

Accommodation

Most of Christchurch's hotels are situated in a reasonably compact central area, though there is a spread of motels through the suburbs. There is also a choice of accommodation near the airport.
(Area code: 03).
Hotels and motels include:
Aalton Motel, 17 Riccarton Road, suburban (tel: 348 6700). 10 units, motel style.
Admiral Motel, 168 Bealey Avenue, near central area (tel: 379 3554). Nine units, motel.
Airport Plaza, at airport (tel: 358 3139). 155 rooms, first class.
Ashleigh Court Motel, 47 Matai Street West, suburban (tel: 348 1888). 12 units. Gold chain.
Autolodge Motor Inn, 72 Papanui Road, midway to the airport (tel: 355 6109). 74 rooms, good standard. Flag chain.
Camelot Court, 28 Papanui

Road, two miles (3km) out (tel: 355 9124). 50 units, motel. Best Western chain.

Coachman, 316 Riccarton Road, suburban (tel: 348 6651). Nine units, motel style.

Latimer Lodge, 30 Latimer Square, central (tel: 379 6760). 53 units, good standard.

Noahs, corner of Worcester and Oxford Terrace, central (tel: 379 4700). 208 rooms, first class.

Pacific Park, 263 Bealey Avenue, near central area (tel: 379 8660). 66 units, good standard.

Parkroyal Hotel, corner of Durham and Kilmore Streets (tel: 365 7799). 297 rooms, first class.

Quality Inn, corner of Durham and Kilmore Streets, central (tel: 365 4699). 161 rooms, first class.

The Russley, Roydvale Avenue, near the airport (tel: 358 8289). 60 rooms, good standard.

For budget accommodation try:
Amber Park, 308 Blenheim Road, three miles (5km) south (tel: 348 3327); campsites and tourist flats.

Top-notch Parkroyal Hotel

Croydon House, 63 Armagh Street, central (tel: 366 5111). 26 rooms, bed and breakfast.

Meadow Park, 39 Meadow Street, three miles (5km) north (tel: 352 9176); campsites and cabins.

Russley Park, 372 Yaldhurst Road, suburban (tel: 342 7021); campsites and tourist flats.

Windsor House, 52 Armagh Street, central (tel: 366 1503). 40 rooms, bed and breakfast.

Restaurants
Many of the accommodation houses mentioned above feature restaurants.
Other restaurants include:
Boaters, Town Hall, central; overlooking Avon river; Mediterranean.

Il Felice, 56 Lichfield Street, central; dinners Italian style.

Ridge Restaurant, up Mount Cavendish gondola (see page 55). Lunch and dinner with views.

Sign of the Takahe, Dyers Pass Road; fine dining with city views.

Strawberry Fare, 114 Peterborough Street, central; dessert menu and light meals.

Thomas Edmonds, 230 Cambridge Terrace; smorgasbord in an old band rotunda.

Wardinskis, The Shades, Cashel Mall, central; café-style brasserie.

Cobb & Co, McDonalds and **Pizza Hut** are in various locations.

Entertainment and Nightlife
Much of Christchurch's entertainment is sport based. The city is proud of **Queen Elizabeth II Park**, which has a

Shop in style in one of the city's malls

stadium and swimming pools originally built for the 1974 Commonwealth Games. The QE complex, which now includes a leisure centre with boats and mini-golf, rollercoaster, swimming pools and squash courts is five miles (8km) from the city centre. Christchurch is also proud of its **Town Hall** next to the Avon in Kilmore Street, which has two auditoria and a restaurant. There are often concerts and recitals here. Look too to see what is on at the **Court Theatre**, one of New Zealand's most important theatre companies. The **Southern Regional Ballet** is based at the Arts Centre. There is live evening entertainment at the **Firehouse Nightclub**. The **Palladium** in Chancery Lane is a vibrant electric disco.

Shopping

Christchurch has an interesting selection of downtown shops spreading out in all directions from its central square. A couple of streets, and the Square itself, are closed to traffic. Parts of Cashel and High Streets are downtown pedestrianised shopping malls. Two department stores of note are **Ballantynes** (in Colombo Street) and **Arthur Barnetts** (in Cashel Street).

In the downtown area look for the **Triangle Centre**, the **Guthrey Centre**, the **Canterbury Centre**, and the **National Mutual Arcade**. There are suburban shopping centres at Merivale and Riccarton.

The 'Canterbury' brand of clothing – multi-coloured sportswear – is a popular buy, downtown at **DF Souvenirs** and at the **Windmill Centre** in Riccarton. There are also souvenir-type shops selling sheepskin, leatherware, wood carvings, and other mementoes.

Information: Christchurch–Canterbury Information Centre, 75 Worcester Street and corner of Oxford Terrace (tel: (03) 379 9629). The AA is at 210 Hereford Street (tel: (03) 379 1280).

THE NORTH OF SOUTH ISLAND

WHAT TO SEE IN THE NORTH OF SOUTH ISLAND

◆
ARTHUR'S PASS
90 miles (146km) northwest of Christchurch
The small township of Arthur's Pass is named after a pass through the Southern Alps, and is surrounded by a National Park of the same name. The pass crosses the Main Divide at an altitude of 3,020 feet (920m). The scenery is quite magnificent, but the road is prohibited for caravans, trailers and vehicles over 42½ feet (13m) long.

The **Arthur's Pass National Park** offers walking tracks and mountain climbing. There is a skifield in the Park (Temple Field). The Park ranges in altitude from 800 feet (245m) to 7,875 feet (2,400m), and the range of scenery is as great – mountain peaks, rushing rivers, glaciers and forest.

The railway line from Christchurch to Greymouth goes via Arthur's Pass and through an electrified tunnel under the Southern Alps. There is a daily return train service, the **Tranz-Alpine Express**, used by many visitors, who travel from Christchurch to Greymouth and back to see the spectacular river and alpine scenery on the route.

Accommodation
At Arthur's Pass there is one motel, **The Alpine** (tel: (03) 318 9233) and one Swiss-style guest house – **The Chalet** (tel: (03) 318 9236), Arthur's Pass. Reserve ahead, as it is a long way to other hotels.

◆◆◆
FOX AND FRANZ JOSEF GLACIERS ✓

about 250 miles (400km) west of Christchurch
These two glaciers – the largest out of 60 in Westland National Park on the west of South Island – and their respective communities are 14 miles (23km) apart by hilly road. Both glaciers are unique in descending as low as 1,000 feet (300m) in temperate zones, and into rainforest. The glaciers are currently advancing, but the general movement over the last half century has been back.

The 7½-mile (12km) **Franz Josef Glacier** was named after the Emperor of Austria by its European discoverer. Access to the face involves a tramp, over river stones and shingle, of up to one hour each way. You can join a guided party for venturing on to the ice. **Don't do it alone.**

The **Fox Glacier** is eight miles (13km) long. From the car park, it is a half-hour walk up the river shingles to where you can 'touch' the glacier. Guided tours are available. From a point two miles (3km) up the approach road, there is a 30-minute walk to a chalet lookout over the glacier.

Lake Matheson, some three miles (5km) from the Fox Glacier township, is renowned for its reflections of the Alps in the water – best in early morning. It is a bush walk of 20 minutes. The road across the Clearwater Flats to Gillespies Beach (where gold was once mined) also provides great vistas of the main range of the Southern Alps falling steeply down to the west coast. Scenic flights in light aircraft are available from both Franz and Fox over both glaciers and alpine areas. South from the glaciers, the Westland road leads down towards the **Haast Pass**, a picturesque lowland pass through the Alps to the southern lakes area of Wanaka and Queenstown.

Accommodation

There is motel accommodation at both Fox and Franz Josef townships. The **Franz Josef Glacier Hotel** (tel: (03) 752 0719) in Westland National Park is adjacent to the little township. Other possibilities at Franz Josef are the **Westland Motor Inn** (tel: (03) 752 0728), or the **Glacier Gateway Motor Lodge**, Highway 6 (tel: (03) 752 0776). The **Fox Glacier Motel** (tel: (03) 751 0804) and the **Golden Glacier Motor Inn** (tel: (03) 751 0847) are at Fox. There are motorcamps at both Fox and Franz Josef.

Information: Fox Glacier Visitor Centre, Highway 6 (tel: (03) 751 0807). Franz Josef Visitor Centre, Highway 6 (tel: (03) 752 0797).

◆

GREYMOUTH
154 miles (248km) west of Christchurch
Greymouth is the largest town along the South Island's west coast. Situated at the mouth of the Grey River, it is a small port and fishing centre. There are

road and rail connections to Christchurch – the scenic rail connection via the Tranz-Alpine Express being a popular trip. Greymouth has developed and survived from its boom days of gold, coal and timber. Its leading attraction is **Shantytown**, a 19th-century gold mining town re-created with buildings brought in from other parts of Westland. The site is signposted 12 miles (20km) south of Greymouth. *Open*: daily 08.30–17.00hrs. Admission charge. Following the Grey River inland leads to remnants and relics of small mining towns – gold and coal – which nature seems to be reclaiming. Some 29 miles (47km) north of Greymouth, **Punakaiki's**

The easy way to visit a glacier

Pancake Rocks and Blowholes, vividly display the ocean's effect on stratified limestone rocks. Inland is the **Paparoa National Park** with canyons, caves and lush vegetation.

Accommodation and Restaurants

Hotel and motel accommodation includes **Ashley Motor Inn**, 70–74 Tasman Street (tel: (03) 768 5135), and **Charles Court Motel**, 350 Main South Road, South Beach (tel: (03) 762 6619). For campers there is the **Greymouth Seaside Holiday Park**, 2 Chesterfield Street (tel: (03) 768 6618). Dine at **Cafe College**, or at the **Ashley**.

Information: Greymouth Information Office, corner of McKay and Herbert Streets (tel: (03) 768 5101).

◆
HOKITIKA
25 miles (40km) south of Greymouth
Founded in 1864, Hokitika had a population of 50,000 by 1866, mostly gold diggers attracted by the newly discovered goldfields in the area. Today greenstone is Hokitika's main product. A kind of nephrite jade, greenstone is still in demand today for jewellery and decorative souvenirs. There are two greenstone factory-shops and other excellent craft shops. The **West Coast Historical Museum** has displays on the goldrush period and pioneer life.
Open: daily 09.30–17.00hrs.

Beyond the town the attraction is scenery. **Lakes Mahinapua** and **Kaniere** offer local walks.

Accommodation and Restaurants

In Hokitika choose motel accommodation such as the **Goldsborough** 252 Revell Street (tel: (03) 755 8773), or the **Hokitika Motel**, 221 Fitzherbert Street (tel: (03) 755 8292). There is a campground. For dining consider the **Tasman View Restaurant**.

Information: Westland Visitor Information Centre, Sewell Street (tel: (03) 755 8322).

◆◆
KAIKOURA
118 miles (191km) north of Christchurch
The rocky Kaikoura Coast, where road and rail routes are squeezed between the Kaikoura range and the sea, is another of New Zealand's scenic delights.

The little town of Kaikoura grew out of a whaling station. Today whales are no longer killed but are again important to the area's economy, as Kaikoura promotes itself as a kind of whale-watchers' centre. Huge sperm whales inhabit the bay off shore and you can take local launch trips to spot them.

The main road by-passes much of the town on its little bluff, from which there are fine seaward views, as well as impressive inland views of the Kaikoura Range sweeping down to the sea. The Peninsula Walkway (3½ hours in all) takes in these views, and also a seal colony.

The **Kaikoura Historical Society** in Ludstone Road has a collection of relics, including whaling items.
Open: weekends 14.00–16.00hrs.
Fyffe House in Avoca Street, is an 1860s whaler's home, now maintained by the Historic Places Trust.
Open: daily, times vary.
The **Kaikoura Aquarium** is open for public viewing.

Accommodation and Restaurants

You could stay at **Alpine View**, 146 Beach Street (tel: (03) 319 5429), or the **Kaikoura Motel**, 11-15 Beach Road (tel: (03) 319 5999). There are also four campgrounds.

When you are hungry, look for **The Cray Pot** restaurant or the **Caves Restaurant** for seafood delicacies of the region – 'Kaikoura' means 'to eat crayfish' (rock lobster) in the Maori language.

Information: Kaikoura Information Centre, The Esplanade (tel: (03) 319 5641).

◆◆
NELSON

272 miles (438km) north of Christchurch

Nelson is the South Island's northernmost city, lying on a stretch of water called Nelson Haven, protected by a natural breakwater from Tasman Bay. The city centre is surrounded and sheltered by hills. Nelson is one of the claimants for New Zealand's sunshine record. It is the commercial centre of a rich horticultural – particularly fruit-growing – region.

The Dutch navigator Abel Tasman visited the area in 1642, but did not land. European settlement began in 1841. In 1857 Nelson's development was stimulated by the discovery of gold inland. **Christ Church Cathedral**

Punakaiki's Pancake Rocks

SOUTH ISLAND : THE NORTH

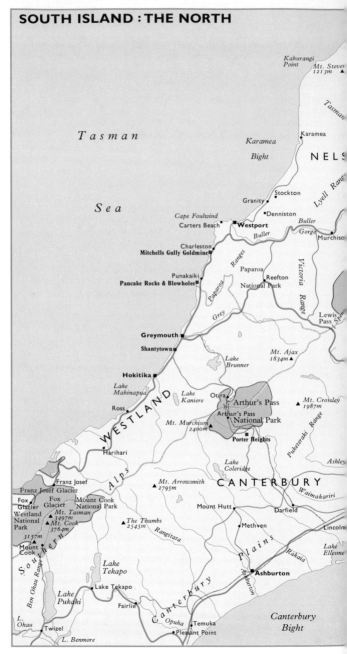

Tasman

Kahurangi
Point

▲ *Mt. Stever*
1213m

Tasman

Karamea
Bight

• Karamea

NELS

Sea

• Stockton

Granity •

• Denniston

Lyell Rang

Cape Foulwind •

• Carters Beach

■ **Westport**

Buller
Gorge

• Murchiso

Charleston •

Buller

Mitchells Gully Goldmine ■

Punakaiki •

Paparoa
Ranges

Reefton ■

Victoria
Range

Pancake Rocks & Blowholes ■

National Park

Lewis
Pass

Paparoa

Grey

Greymouth ■

Shantytown ■

Lake
Brunner

▲ *Mt. Ajax*
1834m

Hokitika ■

Lake
Mahinapua

Lake
Kaniere

Otira •

Arthur's Pass

Ross •

Arthur's Pass
National Park

▲ *Mt. Crossley*
1987m

WESTLAND

▲ *Mt. Murchison*
2400m

Porter Heights ■

Puketeraki
Range

Harihari •

Lake
Coleridge

Ashley

Alps

▲ *Mt. Arrowsmith*
2795m

CANTERBURY

Waimakariri

• Franz Josef

Franz Josef Glacier

Fox
Glacier •

Fox
Glacier

Mount Cook
National Park

• Mount Hutt

• Darfield

Westland
National
Park

▲ *Mt. Tasman*
3497m
▲ *Mt. Cook*
376.m

▲ *The Thumbs*
2545m

• Methven

Rangitata

Lincoln

3157m

Plains

Lake
Ellesme

Mount
Cook

Southern Range

Lake
Tekapo

Rakaia

Ben Ohau Range

• Lake Tekapo

Ashburton ■

L.
Ohau

Lake
Pukaki

• Fairlie

Canterbury

Canterbury
Bight

Twizel

L. Benmore

• Opuha

• Temuka

• Pleasant Point

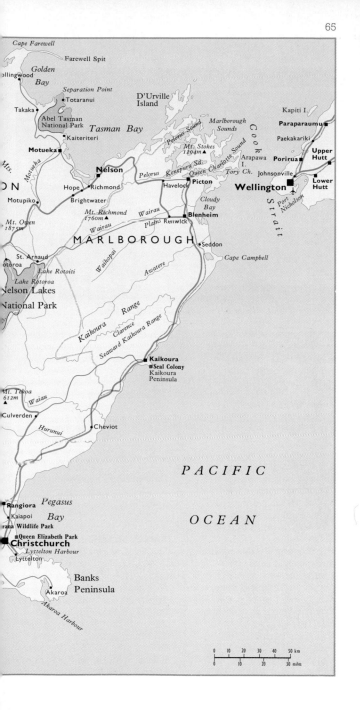

Cape Farewell
Farewell Spit
Golden Bay
ollingwood
Separation Point
Takaka
Totaranui
Abel Tasman National Park
Kaiteriteri
D'Urville Island
Tasman Bay
Motueka
Mtss.
Motueka
ON
Motupiko
Hope
Richmond
Brightwater
Nelson
Pelorus
Marlborough Sounds
Pelorus Sound
Mt. Stokes 1204m▲
Kenepuru Sd.
Queen Charlotte Sound
Havelock
Picton
Arapawa I.
Tory Ch.
Cook Strait
Kapiti I.
Paraparaumu
Paekakariki
Porirua
Upper Hutt
Johnsonville
Wellington
Lower Hutt
Mt. Richmond 1760m▲
Wairau
Wairau
Cloudy Bay
Blenheim
Port Nicholson
Mt. Owen 1875m
Wairau Plains
Renwick
MARLBOROUGH
Seddon
St. Arnaud
otoroa
Lake Rotoiti
Lake Rotoroa
Nelson Lakes National Park
Wahopai
Awatere
Cape Campbell
Kaikoura Range
Clarence
Seaward Kaikoura Range
Mt. Tekoa 612m▲
Waiau
Culverden
Hurunui
Cheviot
Kaikoura
Seal Colony
Kaikoura Peninsula
PACIFIC
Rangiora
Pegasus Bay
Kaiapoi
rana Wildlife Park
Queen Elizabeth Park
Christchurch
Lyttelton Harbour
Lyttelton
OCEAN
Banks Peninsula
Akaroa
Akaroa Harbour

0 10 20 30 40 50 km
0   10   20   30 miles

Trafalgar Street, Nelson

stands on raised ground at the end of Trafalgar Street, with an impressive flight of steps leading up to it. This Anglican cathedral, mostly in marble, was started in 1925. The **Bishop Suter Art Gallery** in the Queens Gardens, Bridge Street, has a well regarded collection of colonial painting.
Open: daily 10.30–16.30hrs.
The **Provincial Museum**, with its historical photographs and Maori collection, is at Isel Park in Stoke, a southern suburb.
Open: Tuesday to Friday, 10.00–16.00 hrs; Saturday and Sunday 14.00–17.00hrs.
The **Queens Gardens** in Bridge Street form an attractive reserve of rare trees and ferns. There is a **Botanical Reserve** in Milton Street, which is reputed to contain the exact centre of New Zealand.
Founders Park is a working museum of re-created buildings and early transport.
Open: daily 10.00–16.30hrs.

Out of Town
Tahunanui Beach, called **Tahuna** for short, is a popular beach with a foreshore sports and play area, three miles (5km) west of the city centre. Another popular beach resort is at **Kaiteriteri** some 40 miles (65km) west of Nelson. It is a safe and scenic bay. From here there are summer launch trips to the **Abel Tasman National Park**, (see page 94). South of Nelson, is the **Nelson Lakes National Park**, consisting of two alpine lakes and the small township of St Arnaud (see also page 95).

Accommodation
The **Quality Inn**, Trafalgar Street (tel: (03) 548 2299), is the city's best hotel. For motor inn accommodation there is **Trailways**, 66 Trafalgar Street (tel: (03) 548 7049), and there are many motels, including the **AA Motor Lodge**, 8-11 Ajax Avenue (tel: (03) 548 8214) and **Balmoral Motor Lodge**, 47 Munitai Street (tel: (03) 548

5018), Tahunanui, three miles (5km) from the city centre.
The **Tahuna Beach Holiday Park**, Beach Road, Tahunanui, offers a big selection of basic tourist flats and cabins as well as campsites.

Restaurants

The restaurants at the Quality Inn and Trailways are a reasonable bet. The **Fisherman's Table** on the waterfront serves seafood. When dining in Nelson you must try Nelson scallops.

Shopping

Nelson has a reputation for arts and crafts, and there are shopping outlets both downtown and out at Tahuna Beach. **Craft Habitat** is a combined studio on Salisbury Road – open every day. Or there is a list of craftspeople available from the Visitor Centre (below).

Information: Nelson Visitor Centre, corner of Trafalgar and Halifax Streets (tel: (03) 548 2304).

◆◆
PICTON

217 miles (350km) north of Christchurch
Picton, at the northwest corner of the South Island, in the recesses of Queen Charlotte Sound, is a good base for exploring the picturesque waterways forming the drowned valley system known as the **Marlborough Sounds**. There are three or four inter-island ferries each way per day between Picton and Wellington, and the trip gives an insight into the scenery of the Sounds. If you are not taking the ferry then you should at least take a launch cruise. The few roads reaching to the outermost stretches of the Sounds are rough and not recommended. The car ferry service to Wellington is operated by Intercity railways. It is usually essential to book ahead if requiring vehicle accommodation (see **Directory** page 124).

Eighteen miles (28km) south of Picton is the bigger town of **Blenheim**. It has a larger shopping area, and is the centre of the famous Marlborough wine district. Take a wine trail tour – from either Blenheim or Picton.

The *Edwin Fox* is the hulk of a clipper ship built in 1853 for the East India Company, housing a floating maritime museum on the Picton waterfront.
Open: daily 08.30–17.30hrs.
On London Quay, **Picton Museum** has a widely varied local collection, including whaling relics.

Picton is the South Island's ferry port and a popular boating centre

Open: daily 10.00–16.00hrs. Admission charge.

Accommodation and Restaurants

Motels include **Marlin Motel**, 33 Devon Street (tel: (03) 573 6784) (half a mile/1km) from town or **Americano Motels**, 32 High Street (tel: (03) 573 6398) (near the beach and post office). For hotel style, there is the **Wesley Picton Inn**, Waikawa Road (tel: (03) 573 7002). An alternative idea is to stay out on the Sounds. The **Portage Hotel**, Kenepuru Road (tel: (03) 573 4309), Marlborough Sounds, is accessible by launch, and by road. It is situated on the beach front and has many facilities. There are several motorcamps: try the **Blue Anchor Holiday Park**, 64 Waikawa Road (tel: (03) 573 7212), close to the ferry terminal.

The **Americano Restaurant** advertises American and New Zealand cuisine. **Neptunes** restaurant offers seafood. Lunch at the **Portage** with a Sounds cruise *en route* is a pleasant excursion.

Information: Picton Information Centre, Auckland Street (tel: (03) 573 8838).

◆

WESTPORT

223 miles (360km) northwest of Christchurch

Westport is a port on the Buller River on the South Island's northwest coast.

It was the search for gold that started the town, but coal has ensured its continued existence.

The Westport coal is a shiny black bituminous type, with particularly good heating qualities. Westport's leading tourist attraction, **Coaltown Museum**, in Queen Street South, displays photographs and relics of historical and contemporary mining in the area.

Open: daily 09.00–16.30hrs. Admission charge.

Immediately south of Westport (seven miles/12km) is **Cape Foulwind**, a promontory with a lighthouse, a seal colony, and Carters Beach.

About 15 miles (24km) south of Westport, near the few remains of the town of Charleston, is **Mitchells Gully Goldmine**. Here amid historic mining terraces is a restored water-wheel and gold battery.

Open: daily 09.00–16.00hrs. Admission charge.

Accommodation and Restaurants

In the town centre is the **Westport Motor Hotel**, Palmerston Street (tel: (03) 789 7889). For motel style look to the **Ascot Motor Lodge**, 74 Romilly Street (tel: (03) 789 7832), or **Buller Bridge Motel**, The Esplanade (tel: (03) 789 7519). The **Seal Colony Tourist Park** at Carters Beach (tel: (03) 789 8002) has a variety of tourist flats and cabins.

For dining, look for **Cristy's Restaurant** or the **Wagon Wheel Carvery** at Larsens Tavern.

Information: Buller Visitor and Information Centre, 1 Brougham Street (tel: (03) 789 6658).

DUNEDIN AND THE DEEP SOUTH

At the northernmost extremity of the area covered here is New Zealand's highest mountain, Mount Cook, centrepiece of the Mount Cook National Park. Skiers and mountaineers are particularly drawn to this landscape of snow and ice and rugged peaks, but the less intrepid can also enjoy its beauty on gentle bush walks from Mount Cook village. Another spectacular area for scenery is Fiordland in the far southwest, also a National Park – one of the world's biggest. The shore is slashed by great inlets stretching far inland into a region of forest and lakes. Milford Sound is the most famous and most visited of the fiords, most people making the trip there from the resort of Te Anau on its great lake of the same name.

New Zealand's deep south, approaching chilly Antarctic regions, does not have the sort of coastal resorts that attract the jet-set. But in Queenstown, on Lake Wakatipu, it has an alpine lake resort which is the most popular holiday centre of the South Island, full of hotels, cafés, nightclubs and pubs to complement the fine setting and many activities.

A far cry from bustling Queenstown is New Zealand's often forgotten third island. Little Stewart Island, off the end of the South Island, is well off the main tourist track, a bush-covered haven for wildlife. There is more than a touch of Scotland here in the deep south – in the landscapes, in the place names and, most of all, in the region's main city, Dunedin, home to New Zealand's only whisky distillery.

DUNEDIN

If you are strolling down a street where the schoolgirls are wearing tartan kilts, if the people around you are rolling their 'r's when they talk, and perhaps the breeze seems a little chillier than in other parts of New Zealand, then the chances are you are in Dunedin – 'Edinburgh of the South' (Dun Edin was the ancient Gaelic name for Edinburgh). The South Island's second

A jet boat on the Shotover River

largest city lies at the head of Otago Harbour, a long waterway sheltered by the scenic Otago Peninsula.

The founding of Dunedin dates from the 1848 arrival of the first ships of the Otago (Free Church of Scotland) Association, which resulted in a mainly Presbyterian settlement – at least initially. In the 1860s the Otago gold rush brought population and prosperity to Dunedin.

However, the city also built its economic structure on the products of the land and industry. The first shipment of frozen meat was despatched from here to England in 1883; and Dunedin was the site of the first freezing works.

New Zealand's first university was established in Dunedin in 1869 – the original building of 1878 is now preserved.

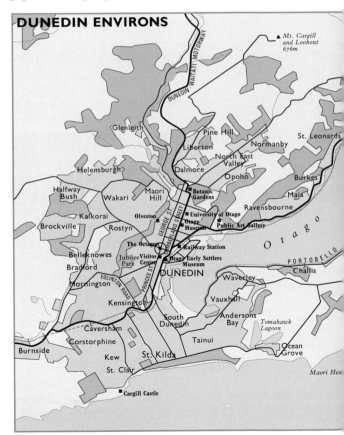

DUNEDIN ENVIRONS

WHAT TO SEE

◆
BOTANIC GARDENS
George Street
These gardens include a rose
walk, the Ellen Terry garden,
Rhododendron Dell (a
wonderful sight in spring),
azalea beds and winter
gardens.
Open: daily during daylight
hours.

◆
DUNEDIN PUBLIC ART GALLERY
Logan Park Drive
Local and imported art is on
show here – including a Monet
– in New Zealand's oldest art
gallery.
Open: Monday to Friday
10.00–17.00hrs; afternoon only
at weekends. Free.

Otago University, at Dunedin

◆
OCTAGON
*between Princes Street and
George Street*
In the centre of the city is this
eight-sided open space, a
popular place to spend
lunchtime. There is a statue of
Scottish poet Robert Burns (who
was the uncle of one of
Dunedin's founding fathers),
and the Town Hall. The big
church there is **St Paul's**
Anglican **Cathedral**, built in
1915. **First Church**, a

Presbyterian Gothic-style edifice, built 1868–73, is only a block away.

◆◆
OLVESTON
42 Royal Terrace
Furnished in keeping with the taste of its original wealthy owner, in 1906, this Jacobean-style homestead is a treasure-house of antiques and *objets d'art*.
Open: daily. There are hour-long tours at set times each day: 09.30, 10.45, 12.00, 13.30, 14.45, 16.00hrs (afternoon only on Sundays). Admission charge.

◆
OTAGO EARLY SETTLERS MUSEUM
220 Cumberland Street
Pioneer relics with photos of settlers and gold mining days, plus an early locomotive and one of Dunedin's former (until 1957) San Francisco-style cable cars, are displayed rather austerely here.
Open: Monday to Friday, 09.00–16.30hrs; Saturday, 10.30–16.30hrs; Sunday, 13.30–16.30hrs. Admission charge.

◆
OTAGO MUSEUM
419 Great King Street
Not only are items from New Zealand, Polynesia and Melanesia displayed here, but ancient civilizations of the Old World are also represented.
Open: as above.

Olveston's Great Hall

◆◆◆
OTAGO PENINSULA
The peninsula guarding Dunedin and its harbour, offers plenty of natural and man-made attractions within easy reach of the city. The Otago Peninsula Trust promotes and preserves its character and wildlife.
Larnach Castle, a kind of Scottish baronial hall, complete with ballroom and battlements, was built in 1871 by a former bank manager and parliamentarian, William Larnach. The castle has spacious grounds.
Open: daily 09.00–17.00hrs. Admission charge.
Glenfalloch Gardens was part of another former homestead. These gardens, at the best in September–October, mix native trees and exotic shrubs, along with peacocks and tea on the terrace.
Open: daily (except Friday afternoon), Admission charge.
Taiaroa Head is the tip of the

Breakers on an Otago beach

peninsula, 18 miles (30km)
from downtown Dunedin. **Fort
Taiaroa** has a 'disappearing
gun' – a six-inch Armstrong
which retracted into the ground
between shots – originally
erected around 1885, now
restored and on display.
Open: daily 10.45–18.45hrs.
Admission charge.
A restricted reserve at Taiaroa
Head is the location of a
Royal Albatross Colony (see
page 95).

◆
RAILWAY STATION
Anzac Avenue
This decorative 1907 building is
now used by only two regular
passenger trains daily. Also
daily, except in winter, a scenic
4-hour train trip operates up the
Taieri Gorge which is highly
recommended.

Out and About
Mount Cargill Lookout is a
2,218-foot (676m) peak, five

miles (8km) out of town, with a
vast panorama over city,
harbour and coast. Another
viewpoint is **Signal Hill**, 1,290
feet (393m), with city and
harbour vistas from suburban
Opoho.
St Kilda is a beach suburb, with
nearby St Clair, offering sports
reserves and the Ocean Beach
steam railway at weekends.

Accommodation
Most good accommodation in
Dunedin is motel style. There is
no deluxe hotel. The following
establishments are
recommended:
Abbey Motor Lodge, 680
Castle Street (tel: (03) 477
5380). 60 units, some motel,
good standard.
Alcala, St Davids Street, north
(tel: (03) 477 9073). 23 units,
good motel. Motor Lodge chain.
Cargills Motor Inn, 678
George Street (tel: (03) 477
7983). 50 rooms, good
standard. Flag chain.
Commodore, 932 Cumberland
Street, north (tel: (03) 477 7766).

THE DEEP SOUTH

Tasman

Sea

Haast

Jackson Head Jackson
Bay
Cascade Point

Mount Aspiring
National Park

Big Bay
Martins Bay

Mount
Aspiring
3027m

Olivine Range

Southern

Lake
Wanaka

Matukituki
Valley

Milford Sound

Mitre Peak
1692m ▲

Milford
Sound

Holyford

Humboldt Mts.

Dart

Rees

Richardson Mts.
2819m

Shotover

Treble Cone ■
Wanaka

Homer
Tunnel
McKinnon Pass

Kinloch

Glenorchy

Mt. Cardrona
1934m ▲

Franklin Mts.

Stuart Mts.

■ Glade House

Coronet Peak ■

Cardrona
Arrowtown

Frankton

Fiordland

Secretary I.

Doubtful Sound

Murchison Mts.

Livingstone Mts.

Queenstown

Lake
Wakatipu

Kawarau

The Remarkables

▲ 2072m

Te Anau
Caves

Lake
Te Anau

National Park

Kepler Mts.

West
Arm

Power Station ■

Lake
Manapouri

▲ **Te Anau**

Marrara

Eyre Mts.

Kingston

Garvie Mts.

Waikaia

Resolution
I.

Manapouri

Takitimu Mts.

L.
Monowai

SOUTHLAND

Lumsden

Cameron Mts.

Lake
Hauroko

Waiau

Aparima

Oreti

Riversdale

Lake
Poteriteri

Otautau

Winton

Gore ■

Mataura

Puysegur
Point

Tuatapere

Te Waewae
Bay

Riverton

Invercargill ■

Toetoes
Bay

Tokanu

Solander I.

Foveaux

Bluff Bluff Harbour
Stirling Pt.

Strait

Codfish I.

Mount Anglem
980m ▲

Mason
Bay

Oban ●

Halfmoon Bay

Paterson Inlet

▲ Mt. Allen
750m

Stewart Island

South West Cape

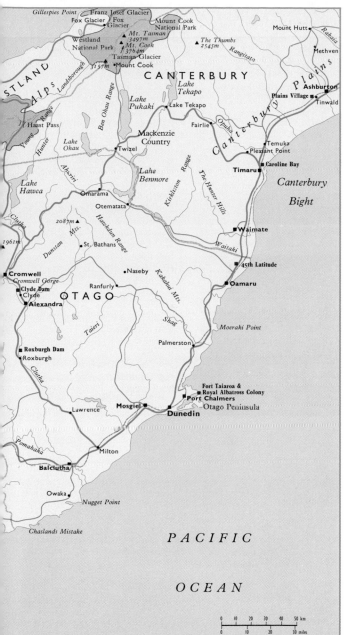

THE DEEP SOUTH

11 units, good motel.
Dunedin Motel and **Academy Court Motel**, 642 George Street, north (tel: (03) 477 7692). 20 units.
Leisure Lodge, Duke Street, half a mile (1km) out in Dunedin North (tel: (03) 477 5360). 76 units, some with cooking.
Quality Inn, Upper Moray Place (tel: (03) 477 6784). 54 rooms, good standard.
Regal Court, 775 George Street, north (tel: (03) 477 7729). 13 units, top class motel.
Southern Cross Hotel, 118 High Street, central (tel: (03) 477 0752). 109 rooms, first class.

For those on a budget:
Aaron Lodge Holiday Park, 162 Kaikourai Valley Road (tel: (03) 476 4725), three miles (5km) out: campsites, cabins and tourist flats.
Leviathan Hotel, corner of High and Cumberland Streets (tel: (03) 477 3160), central. 88 rooms, moderate.

Restaurants

You can eat at some of the hotels listed above. The better hotel restaurants are included in the following list:
Abbeys, Abbey Motor Lodge: buffet lunch and dinners.
Aggies, Pacific Park Hotel: first class NZ cuisine with views.
Cargills, Cargills Motor Inn: French cuisine.
Cobb & Co, Lawcourts Establishment, 53 Lower Stuart Street: family dining.
Clarendons, 28 McLaggard Street, central: in an old hotel building.
Harbour Lights, cafe style, Macandrew Bay, Otago Peninsula.
McDonalds, 232 George Street, central: same here as anywhere.
The Huntsman, 311 George Street, central; chargrill steak house.
Southern Cross Hotel: lobby, restaurant, brasserie and 24-hour café.

Mount Cargill's bracing harbour view

Entertainment and Nightlife

As elsewhere in New Zealand, Dunedin's citizens find much of their entertainment in playing or watching sport.

Dunedin is not a late-night city. Evening meals are generally consumed earlier than in Wellington or Auckland, even though in summer, with the addition of daylight saving, twilight comes late.

Most hotel taverns have live music on Friday and Saturday evenings – try the **Gardens Tavern** or the **Shoreline Motor Inn**. Nightclubs include **Sammy's Cabaret** or **Club Nouveau** (not Monday and Tuesday).

Allen Hall, on the Otago University campus, offers student and touring drama productions. The **Fortune Theatre** in Upper Moray Place, once a church, houses Dunedin's only professional theatre group. The **Globe Theatre** features amateur productions.

Shopping

George Street is the city's main shipping street, with establishments offering a full range of merchandise; there is even a shop selling tartans. **Arthur Barnetts** is Dunedin's leading department store. **Carnegie Centre** in Upper Moray Place houses a number of arts and craft dealers. Books about the settlement of Dunedin and Otago are available at the **Otago Heritage Shop** near the Octagon.

Most city shops are open late until 21.00 hours on Friday nights.

Information: Dunedin Visitor Centre, 48 The Octagon (tel: (03) 474 3300). The AA is at 450 Moray Place (tel: (03) 477 5945).

◆

ALEXANDRA

118 miles (190km) northwest of Dunedin

Located in the somewhat barren region of central Otago, the small town of Alexandra is a gateway to the more spectacular vistas of mountains and southern lakes beyond. Alexandra sits next to the Clutha River – New Zealand's greatest by volume – and the area was the centre of feverish gold mining activity in the 1860s, followed by gold dredging. Today the town is a centre for growers of stone fruit crops. You can still see the piers of the old town bridge (1882), and on Knobbie Range, a hill behind the town, a giant illuminated clock counts the hours. Up Little Valley Road at the **Tucker Hill Lookout**, only a mile (1.6km) out of town, there is an overview of Alexandra and its immediate surroundings.

The **Sir William Bodkin Museum** in Thomson Street has a gold mining collection. *Open*: weekdays 14.00–16.00hrs.

The old **Alexandra Courthouse** in Tarbert Street, built 1876 of schist stone, and the **Vallance Cottage** built of mud bricks, nearly a century ago, near by in Samson Street, are other local buildings of interest. The town hosts a Blossom Festival in the fourth week of September.

A day excursion out of Alexandra takes in the historic

THE DEEP SOUTH

Bluff is renowned for its oysters

old gold towns of **Naseby** and **St Bathans**, to the northeast.

Accommodation and Restaurants

The **Centennial Court Motor Inn**, 96 Centennial Avenue (tel: (03) 448 6482), has both hotel and motel rooms.
Avenue Motel, 119 Centennial Avenue (tel: (03) 448 6918), also offers a good motel-style standard.
Alexandra has two campgrounds.
The Centennial Court has a restaurant. Otherwise, consider the **Bendigo Restaurant and Bar** – an establishment that goes back to the 1880s. Up the road at Clyde you should seek out **Olivers** for food and music in an old stone store.

Information: Central Otago Visitor Information Centre, 28 Centennial Avenue (tel: (03) 448 9515).

◆
INVERCARGILL
135 miles (217km) southwest of Dunedin
Almost at the southern tip of

the South Island, Invercargill is the leading centre for the fertile region of Southland. You know you are in Southland by the concentration of white sheep dotting the green paddocks.
Bluff is the city's port, 19 miles (30km) away – a kind of 'Land's End' – and world famous for its oysters. Behind Bluff, a road rises up **Bluff Hill** to 870 feet (265m) for a view across Bluff Harbour and out on to Foveaux Strait which separates South Island from Stewart Island. Beyond Bluff, a road continues to **Stirling Point**. At this southern outpost a sign indicates distances to other parts of the world.
Founded in 1856, Invercargill has wide streets and pleasant parks and open spaces. Its main tourist attraction is the **Southland Centennial Museum** in Gala Street, which includes items from Southland's history and a display featuring the tuatara – sole living survivor of an ancient group of reptiles. There is also an exhibit which, with audio-visual effects, reproduces a sub-antarctic environment.
Open: weekdays 10.00–16.30hrs; weekends 14.00–17.00hrs.
Nearby **Queens Park** contains formal gardens, winter gardens, sports area, aviary and deer park.
The **City Art Gallery** is in Anderson Park, 4½ miles (7km) out of the city. It houses historic and contemporary art in an old homestead.
Open: 14.00–16.30hrs except Monday and Fridays.

Accommodation

For accommodation in Invercargill head for the **Kelvin Hotel** downtown at 16 Kelvin Street (tel: (03) 218 2829), or the fine **Ascot Park Motor Hotel** (tel: (03) 217 6195), on a 17-acre (7 hectare) site on the corner of Tay Street and Race Course Road, a short distance out of town. The **Townsman Motor Lodge** at 195 Tay Street (tel: (03) 218 8027) and the **Balmoral Lodge** at 265 Tay Street (tel: (03) 217 6109) are two other possibilities. There is a choice of motor camp and caravan parks.

Restaurants

For dining try Ascot Park Motor Hotel or the **Highlights Room** atop the Kelvin. The Old English style **Strathern Inn** has won awards, as has the **Donovan Restaurant** which specialises in New Zealand cuisine. At Stirling Point, past Bluff, the **Stirling Point** is the southernmost restaurant in the South Island.

Information: the Visitor Centre is at 82 Dee Street.

Invercargill's manicured lawns

◆◆◆
MANAPOURI AND TE ANAU
about 180 miles (290km) west of Dunedin

In the southwest corner of the South Island lie Lakes Manapouri and Te Anau, great stretches of water with mountain backdrops, bordering on to the Fiordland National Park (see page 80). And beside each nestles a resort named after its lake. The town of Te Anau is the gateway to the majestic and mountainous Fiordland region, including mighty Milford Sound (see page 81).

Lake Te Anau is the South Island's largest lake, covering 133 square miles (344sq km). Its eastern shoreline is largely developed farmland, but on its western side are three fiords that penetrate into the rugged Fiordland vastness.

Nearby Lake Manapouri, with depths of over 1,300 feet (400m), is New Zealand's deepest lake. In the 1960s a proposal to raise its level and harness it for power generation led to a huge public outcry. The scheme was modified to leave the lake's beauty unimpaired.

Tiny Manapouri township is only 12 miles (19km) from Te Anau. The two towns share an airport. Te Anau is served by regular scheduled coaches.

Lake Trips

There are various Lake Te Anau cruises, including one to **Te Ana-au Caves**, featuring rushing water, an underground waterfall, and glow-worms. Other launch trips operate to

THE DEEP SOUTH

Glade House, the starting point for Milford Track at the top of the lake (see page 82).

On Lake Manapouri the top sightseeing tour starts with a launch cruise across the scenic lake to **West Arm**, where a bus takes you down through a spiral tunnel more than a mile (1.6km) long, to a giant underground powerhouse hewn 700 feet (213m) down inside the mountain. This big hydroelectric power scheme generates electricity for the national grid and for the aluminium smelter at Bluff near Invercargill. The lake waters discharge through a six-mile (10km) tailrace tunnel into the sea at **Doubtful Sound**. (It was Captain Cook who viewed the Sound from the sea in 1770 and was 'doubtful' about its extent.) Some tours also provide a cruise on Doubtful Sound. **Fiordland Travel**, operator of most of the local tourist trips, acts as the Visitor Information Centre (see **Information** below).

Walks

The **Fiordland National Park** is the largest, most rugged, and most remote of the country's park system. Crossed by walking tracks of various difficulty and length, it has an area of about 3 million acres (1.2 million hectares), and a dozen steep walled Sounds where the Tasman Sea infiltrates the mountains. See also **Peace and Quiet**, page 96. For details of some tracks, see **Milford Sound** and **Queenstown**, pages 82 and 86. The **Kepler Track** is a walk of three–four days through the mountain vastness between and beyond the Te Anau and Manapouri lakes – but it is not suitable for the inexperienced walker.

Accommodation

At Te Anau, the **Te Anau Travelodge** (tel: (03) 249 7411) is on the lakefront. The **Village Inn**, Mokoroa Street (tel: (03) 249 7911), built to look like a pioneer village, has many facilities. There are also the **Explorer Motel**, 6 Cleddau Street (tel: (03) 249 7156), and **Aden Motel**, 59 Quintin Drive (tel: (03) 249 7748). All except the Aden have restaurants. At Manapouri, **Lakeview Motor Inn** (tel: (03) 249 6652) has 55 rooms.

There is a choice of camp and caravan parks.

Information: Visitor Information Centre, Fiordland Travel, Te Anau Terrace, Te Anau (tel: (03) 249 7419).

♦♦♦
MILFORD SOUND ✓

*240 miles (387km) northwest of
Dunedin*
Described by Rudyard Kipling
as 'the eighth wonder of the
world', Milford Sound is nine
miles (15km) long, has a
comparatively shallow
entrance, but is deep within. It is
surrounded by mountain cliffs
which rise vertically 4,000 feet
(1,200m) and are laced with
huge waterfalls, dropping sheer
into the sea. A cruise on the
Sound is a tourist must, and
allows you to see spectacular
views of the Bowen Falls,
Stirling Falls and 5,558-foot
(1,694m) Mitre Peak, rising like
a pyramid above the water. A
small airstrip allows local scenic
flights, and also connections to
Te Anau and Queenstown.
Milford Sound is the most
accessible of the Fiordland

*Above: majestic Milford Sound, one
of New Zealand's great sights*

*Below: high point of Milford Track,
a wilderness walk*

fiords at the end of the 74-mile
(119km) road from Te Anau.
One of New Zealand's most
picturesque routes, it takes in
mountain scenery, lakes, a high-
altitude tunnel emerging into
the Welsh-sounding Cleddau
Valley, and a winding descent
to the Sound. The road is now
sealed, but can be subject to
snow or avalanches. Drivers
are urged to pay strict
attention to all signs erected
for their safety. The Homer
Tunnel remains rough-hewn
and unsealed. Drivers unused
to driving on the left, or on
unsealed surfaces, might

consider taking a tour bus from Te Anau, or from Queenstown.

Walks

The **Milford Track** is a four-day walk, much of it through native bush forest, from Glade House at the head of Lake Te Anau through beech forest, over the McKinnon Pass and down the Arthur River to Sandfly Point (which lives up to its name) on Milford Sound. The 1,900-foot (580m) Sutherland Falls, the world's fifth highest, can be visited *en route*. Boat access is required and scheduled at both ends of the track. You may choose between a conducted walk staying overnight at mini-hostels, or a 'freedom' walk staying at Park Board huts. Advance bookings are required for both. Enquire at the Fiordland National Park Visitor Centre at Te Anau.

The **Hollyford Track** goes down the 50-mile (80km) Hollyford Valley to the coast at Martins Bay. There are alternative inclusive packages available, allowing walks one way with flight out, or walking both ways. Options range from three to five days. Contact **Hollyford Tours and Travel**, Queenstown Airport, PO Box 205, Wakatipu.

Accommodation

Accommodation is limited to the **THC Milford Sound Hotel**, Milford Sound (tel: (03) 249 7926), and the hostel style **Milford Sound Lodge**, at Milford Road, Milford Sound (tel: (03) 249 8071), which also has camping facilities. The Milford Hotel has a popular smorgasbord lunch, and a magnificent view of Mitre Peak from its lounge.

◆◆◆
MOUNT COOK ✓

204 miles (329km) northwest of Dunedin

Mount Cook is New Zealand's highest mountain at 12,349 feet (3,764m), and is adjacent to, but not part of, the main divide of the Southern Alps. Its Maori name is Aorangi meaning 'cloud piercer', a good evocation of the mountain's pyramidal shape, easily recognised from afar.

The name Mount Cook also applies to the resort settlement situated among the grand alpine scenery (also known as The Hermitage, after its leading hotel).

There are daily coach and air services linking Mount Cook with Christchurch and Queenstown.

Surrounding the village is **Mount Cook National Park**, over 173,000 acres (70,000 hectares) of mountain, valley and glacier scenery.

The National Park has a Visitor Centre and there are numerous walking tracks – though the terrain is more suitable for serious climbers than for walkers. Flights in ski-equipped light aircraft are popular, taking in views of Mount Cook and the Alps, and including a landing on the snowfield of the **Tasman Glacier**.

This glacier, 18 miles (29km) long, is the longest of any in the world's temperate zones. Skiers can fly to the snowfields at the

Lake scenery in the southern Alps

top for skiing, but there are no ski facilities.

Scenic flights also cross the Southern Alps to the Franz Josef and Fox Glaciers on the other side (see page 60).

Accommodation

The **Hermitage**, Mount Cook, is the leading hotel, but the **Mount Cook Travelodge** and **Mount Cook Chalets** provide alternative standards. All three share the same telephone (03) 435 1809. The Hermitage has two restaurants and a coffee shop. Camping is available at **Glentanner Park**, State Highway 80, Clentanner, (tel: (03) 435 1855) 14 miles (23km) away near Lake Pukaki.

Information: Mount Cook National Park Visitor Centre, Bowen Drive (tel: (03) 435 1818).

◆

OAMARU

71 miles (115km) north of Dunedin

Six miles (10km) north of Oamaru is a roadside plaque recording a spot mid-way on the 45th latitude between the Equator and the South Pole. A pastoral, commercial and distribution centre for the northern Otago region, Oamaru is best known for its stone, used for public buildings throughout New Zealand. The white limestone can be cut with hand saws when freshly quarried, but it hardens with age.

Many of Oamaru's older limestone buildings still look grand and impressive. The **National Bank** and **Bank of New South Wales** buildings were erected in 1870 and 1884 respectively. The latter, in Thames Street, is now the **Forrester Art Gallery**. Also look for the 'old' (1864) and 'new' (1884) Post Offices. The long-established **Oamaru Gardens**, in Severn Street near the town centre, are exceptional, with garden displays, statuary and an aviary among other delights. Some 14 miles (22km) north of the town, the Waitaki River forms a historical boundary between

THE DEEP SOUTH

the Christchurch/Canterbury and Dunedin/Otago regions, linking them with a bridge over 3,000 feet (1,000m) long.

Accommodation and Restaurants

Oamaru accommodation is mainly motel style. You could consider the **Heritage Court Motor Lodge**, 346 Thames Highway (tel: (03) 437 2200), with good facilities, or the **Colonial Lodge Motel**, 509 Thames Highway (tel: (03) 437 0999).

Dine in the **Wanbrow Room** at the old Brydone Hotel, or consider the **Last Post** restaurant.

Shopping and Information:

The main shopping street, and location of the Oamaru Information Centre (tel: (03) 434 5643), is Severn Street.

Queenstown on Lake Wakatipu

◆◆◆
QUEENSTOWN ✓

175 miles (283km) northwest of Dunedin

Without a doubt, the liveliest and most popular resort of the South Island is cosmopolitan Queenstown.

The town rises gently above the blue waters of **Lake Wakatipu**, the South Island's second largest lake, and is backed by the majestic Remarkables mountain range. Queenstown has good transport links by air and bus, and coach tours operate through the town. There is a huge choice of activities available if you stay in Queenstown. On the lake, you can, for instance, cruise, sail or windsurf; while on the neighbouring rivers, you can jet boat or go white water rafting. There is skiing in the mountains in winter and hiking in the hinterland. And to see everything at once, you can take a sightseeing flight. To match its international image, Queenstown has more of a night scene to offer than the majority of New Zealand resorts, with good dining and live entertainment.

Out and About

The **TSS** *Earnslaw*, the 'lady of the lake', makes daily cruises. This 1912 coal-burning steamship used to be very much a workhorse, carrying sheep and general cargo. Its passage around the lake is controversially marked by its black smoke. There are many other lake trips – around to Frankton Arm or across the lake to have morning or afternoon tea at one of the high country sheep stations: Walter Peak, or Mount Nicholas. You may also see a sheepdog, sheep-shearing or wool-spinning display.

Back on land the **Skyline Gondola**, a short walk from downtown, lifts people in little cablecars 1,445 feet (440m) up the cableway to Bobs Peak for dramatic views over the town, lake and mountains. There is a restaurant at the top.

At the base of the gondola in Brecon Street, is the **Queenstown Motor Museum** for car enthusiasts (vintage, veteran and classic machines). *Open*: daily 09.00–17.30hrs.

Coronet Peak is a leading ski resort from June to October (approximately), but it is worth visiting at any time of the year. Road's end, with facilities, is about nine miles (15km) out of town, but from there a chairlift takes you to the peak at 5,413 feet (1,650m). From the Coronet Peak road, a side road branches to **Skippers Canyon**. This narrow road, built during the gold rush, has precipitous sides and clifts, and it is the thrill of the journey that is its attraction.

Experienced drivers only should attempt it; you might prefer a tour by minibus. Rental cars and motorhomes may not be driven on this road.

It was the gold rush of 1862 that brought people into the area – to Queenstown and, especially, to **Arrowtown**, 12½ miles (20km) away, Arrowtown's main thoroughfare, Buckingham Street, still retains the savour of

Take your pick from the choice of attractions

old goldmining days in its shops and pubs – and souvenir sellers.

The **Lakes District Centennial Museum**, towards the end of the main street, houses a collection of gold mining relics and other memorabilia from the Wakatipu area. *Open*: daily 09.00–17.00hrs.

Arrowtown has an autumn festival, a combination of colours and heritage, in the third week of April.

The road to Arrowtown crosses a bridge over the **Shotover River**, the golden waterway that, further upriver, threads the Skippers Canyon. From that bridge you can watch jet boats ride the river, and then go down for a ride yourself.

Jet boats were a New Zealand invention, using a special water propulsion system to enable small boats to skilfully navigate shallow waters. Jet boats are used in many parts of New Zealand as a means of transport and reasonably fast sightseeing, but in the Queenstown district the drivers' skills provide thrill rides through narrow gorges. The Shotover Jet seems to be

THE DEEP SOUTH

A Queenstown landmark

the most popular of several options. The operators provide connecting transport from Queenstown.

The road to the head of Lake Wakatipu (unsealed and very dusty) is also a scenic one, but from this head of the lake area you have to take to your feet, and there are several tramping tracks of note.

Tracks

The 24-mile (39km) **Routeburn Track** is typically a three- or four-day walk over the mountains to the Hollyford Valley on the Milford Sound Road. You can choose between guided tours overnighting at mini-hostels, or 'freedom' walking to overnight at park board huts – if there is room! For more details, enquire at one of the information centres in Queenstown.

Alternative walks are the **Greenstone Track** and the **Caples Track**, both linking through to the Hollyford Valley.

In summer there are bus connections from Queenstown to the start of the tracks. All three tracks are through forest, with mountain views and some steep slopes, though the paths are well defined. Expect rain at any time even though the walks are usually done in summer only – say November to May. The Routeburn can be blocked by snow at other times.

Other tourist options in the Queenstown area include the **Kingston Flyer** (a steam train trip, with staff in period costume, operating only in summer from Kingston at the southern end of Lake Wakatipu).

Accommodation

The **Holiday Inn** in Sainsbury Road, Fernhill (tel: (03) 442 6600), and the **Gardens Parkroyal** (tel: (03) 442 7750) on the corner of Marine Parade and Earl Street, near the town wharf, vie for the top of the accommodation market.

In the middle range are the **A-Line Hotel**, overlooking Queenstown Bay at 27 Stanley Street (tel: (03) 442 7700), and the **Lakeland Hotel**, Lake Esplanade (tel: (03) 442 7600), with beautiful views. **Mountain View Lodge**, half a mile (1km) from the town centre in Frankton Road (tel: (03) 442 8246), **Blue Peaks Lodge**, on the corner of Stanley and Sydney Streets (tel: (03) 442 9224) offer hotel and motel rooms.

For campers, the **Queenstown Motor Park** on Mann street (tel: (03) 442 7252) has good location and facilities.

Restaurants

The above hotels have restaurants, but there are plenty of eating alternatives. The **Gantley's Restaurant**, out of town at Arthur's Point, has a good name for New Zealand cuisine, while in town **The Cow** in Cow Lane has a reputation for the best pizzas. About ten eating options are available in the Food Hall of **O'Connells Pavilion**; while the **Skyline** restaurant, atop the gondola cableway, you can dine with a view. And on the lake, the **TSS** *Earnslaw* offers lunch and dinner trips, with a carvery and piano.

Nightlife

Nightlife in Queenstown varies with the seasons – from *après-ski* in winter when it is dark and cold to lively summer nights when daylight saving delays the dusk until 22.00 hours or so. Lakefront **Eichardt's Tavern** is lively whatever the season, and has a disco upstairs.
There is entertainment every night at **Chico's**, in the Mall.

Shopping

Queenstown has a compact central shopping area, and its main street is a pedestrian mall. Many businesses are open daily, until late in summer, though sometimes closing for a dinner hour.
Local arts and crafts – including greenstone jewellery and Maori carvings – together with a wide range of New Zealand souvenirs, such as sheepskin, wool, leather and suede goods, are available.

Information: Visitor Information Centre, InterCity Travel (Queenstown) Ltd, corner of Shotover and Camp Streets (tel: (03) 442 8238).

◆
STEWART ISLAND

Stewart Island, tiny though it is (66 square miles/172sq km), is New Zealand's third main island. It lies off the south end of the South Island across the Foveaux Strait. The Island is well forested, has a heavy rainfall, and a highest point of 3,215 feet (980m) in Mount Anglem. It is a naturalists' paradise.
The township of **Oban** (population 340) on Halfmoon Bay off Paterson Inlet, is the only settled area, with a port and airstrip. Roads on the island are limited, and mostly unsealed. Accommodation is also limited. Access to the island is by air from Invercargill, or by catamaran from Bluff.
See also **Peace and Quiet**, page 97

Information: Stewart Island Visitor Centre, Main Road, Half Moon Bay (tel: (03) 219 1218).

◆
TIMARU

123 miles (199km) north of Dunedin
A whaling station was established near the present site of Timaru, on the east coast at the edge of the Canterbury Plains, in 1837. A town was laid out in 1857, and the first real settlers arrived in 1859. A fire destroyed much of the early town in 1868. Two of Timaru's

THE DEEP SOUTH

heroes, from earlier this century, are the aviator Richard Pearse, who possibly beat the Wright brothers into the air and certainly made New Zealand's first powered flight in 1903, and the racehorse Phar Lap, a champion of Australian and US race courses in the 1920s and 1930s.

Caroline Bay just north of the port is a sandy beach with facilities such as mini-golf and tennis courts. An unusual Christmas/New Year carnival is held here – an event which draws visitors from all over New Zealand with competitions, entertainments, fireworks and, as a grand finale, New Year's Eve bonfire.

The **Botanical Gardens**, situated between Queen Street and King Street, just south of the main shopping area in Timaru, is a pleasant and relaxing retreat featuring extensive gardens and wild reserves, as well as glasshouses and a fernery.

The **South Canterbury Hall Museum** in Perth Street has a collection of pioneer relics, Maori artefacts, and photographs of port development.

Open: Tuesday to Friday 13.30-16.30hrs; weekends 13.30–16.00hrs. Admission free.

The **Aigantighe Art Gallery** in Wai-iti Road features a local permanent collection and occasionally includes touring exhibitions.

Open: Tuesday to Friday 11.00 to 16.30hrs; weekends 14.00–16.30hrs. Admission free.

Accommodation and Restaurants

Close to the city centre is the **Trailways Motor Inn** (tel: (03) 688 4049). **Seabreeze Motel**, at 364 Stafford Street (tel: (03) 684 3119), overlooks Caroline Bay and has good facilities.

Campers should look for the **Selwyn Holiday Park** at 8 Glen Street (tel: (03) 684 7690), at the northern end of town. It has tourist flats and cabins.

There is a family restaurant in the Hibernian Hotel or try the **Richard Pearse Restaurant** at The Tavern in Le Cren Street.

Information: South Canterbury/Timaru Information Centre, 14 George Street (tel: (03) 688 6163).

◆◆
WANAKA
171 miles (276km) northwest of Dunedin

This popular southern lakes resort on the shore of Lake Wanaka has retained the flavour of a typical New Zealand holiday town – in contrast with swinging, cosmopolitan Queenstown. Lake Wanaka is one of the South Island's largest lakes, beautifully placed among mountains and popular for all kinds of watersports. There is skiing in winter at nearby **Cardrona** and **Treble Cone** Ski Areas – the latter for the more experienced.

The **War Memorial Lookout**, above the town in Chalmers Street, provides a view over the locality and lake.

The world's first three-dimensional maze – the **Great**

The peak of Mount Aspiring in the Southern Alps

Maze – is a popular attraction just about a mile (1.6km) out of town. It takes an average 40 minutes to sort out the lanes, underpasses and bridges of this teaser. There is more in the **Puzzle Centre** located next door, where many different sorts of puzzles are demonstrated and sold.
Open: daily 08.30–17.30hrs. Admission charge.
Glendhu Bay, seven miles (11km) around the lake, is a favourite place for scenic views, especially in autumn. The **Mount Aspiring National Park**, northeast of Wanaka, is a largely undeveloped section of the Southern Alps surrounding the 9,931-foot (3,027m) peak of Mount Aspiring. The park is a wilderness area for trampers and climbers, with little road access. The road up the Matukituki Valley offers scenic views, but the surface deteriorates beyond 25 miles (40km), or so. There is a Park Visitor Centre at Ardmore Street, in Wanaka, which is recommended. See also **Peace and Quiet** page 96.

Accommodation and Restaurants
The **Edgewater Resort** (tel: (03) 443 8311) is an up-market establishment in Sargood Drive in the town centre with 95 rooms. The **Wanaka Motor Inn** is on Mount Aspiring Road (tel: (03) 443 8216). For motel style accommodation, consider the **Fairway Lodge**, Highway 89 (tel: (03) 443 7285), or the **Bay View Motel**, Glendhu Bay Road (tel: (03) 443 7766). Campers should look for the **Pleasant Lodge Holiday Park**, Mount Aspiring Road (tel: (03) 443 7360).
For eating try **Capriccio Trattoria** in the shopping centre, or **Rafters** on the Mount Aspiring Road.

Information: Wanaka Visitor Information Centre, Ardmore Street (tel: (03) 443 1233).

PEACE AND QUIET

Countryside and Wildlife in New Zealand

by Paul Sterry

New Zealand is a land of extraordinary variety and beauty: few other countries can boast such a range of habitats within such a comparatively small area. Although it occupies an area barely larger than Great Britain, everything from alpine scenery and sub-tropical forests to coastal fiords, scrub and grasslands, and rivers and wetlands can be found in New Zealand.

The wildlife is also rich and varied. Apart from several introduced species, many of the plants and animals are unique and endemic. There are no native ground-dwelling mammals – New Zealand became separated from other land masses before mammals could reach it – and as a consequence, some of the birds are now flightless, since they evolved when there were no predatory ground mammals. They have also evolved to occupy many of the 'niches' – such as pollination and seed dispersal – normally associated with insects and mammals elsewhere.

Farming practices and deforestation have taken a heavy toll of the natural vegetation – less than 25 per cent of the country is now wooded, whereas about 80 per cent was estimated to have been covered prior to man's arrival. However, 12 national parks, 20 forest parks, 3 maritime parks and numerous reserves safeguard some of the best remaining areas and harbour some of the finest scenery in the world as well as some of the most extraordinary creatures.

In and Around Auckland

In the city itself, the Tahuna Torea Nature Reserve, which lies on the Glendowie Spit at the Tamaki River, gives a good introduction to New Zealand wildlife, with several species of native birds being easily seen. Elsewhere, in parks and gardens, visitors from Europe will be intrigued to see birds more familiar on their home territory – blackbirds, song thrushes, goldfinches, greenfinches, starlings and the inevitable house sparrow. Among the best places to explore are the Wintergardens in Auckland City Centre, and the Coast-to-Coast Walkway which starts at the Ferry Building.

Two coastal areas of estuary

Forests edge Lake Tarawera

and mudflats lie close to Auckland and are well worth visiting. The Firth of Thames, best viewed from Miranda, is to the east and is bordered by the Coromandel Peninsula, itself well worth exploring for its rugged terrain and native forests (see page 34). Manukau Harbour, best viewed from the south side, lies to the south of the city. Careful note of the state of the tide will help get the most from both spots: at low tide, the birds are often distant, feeding out on the mudflats, while on a rising tide they are pushed closer and closer to the shore. Species likely to be seen include wrybills, delightful waders whose bill tip is bent to the right halfway along its length. Wrybills are only found in New Zealand, breeding on shingle ridges on inland rivers. By travelling north from Auckland into the Northland, visitors can reach excellent sites such as Whangarei Harbour, home to breeding New Zealand dotterels and a wide variety of non-breeding waders. Waitangi State forest is worth exploring, and there is even a chance of seeing a kiwi here. This flightless and, in some areas, threatened species, is, of course, New Zealand's national bird. The Waipoua Forest Sanctuary within Northland State Forest Park harbours remnants of the once extensive kauri forests that formerly cloaked the region. A cone-bearing species, the kauri is extremely long-lived and some specimens may be more than 1,500 years old.

Little Barrier Island

Man's influence has even spread to New Zealand's offshore islands, where cats and rats take a heavy toll on sea birds, and where grazing animals have destroyed much of the vegetation. However, Little Barrier Island still remains forested and virtually unspoilt.

Stitchbird

The stitchbird belongs to a family of birds called honeyeaters. As that name suggests, they feed on nectar gathered from flowers, and are assisted in this process by a brush-like tongue. Stitchbirds also feed on insects and fruit. They are about eight inches (20cm) long and have a warbler-like appearance, with a prominent white wing bar. Males have a black hood with a white streak behind the eye. Once widespread across most of the North Island and some of the offshore islands, stitchbirds are now restricted to the forests of Little Barrier Island, where they are quite common.

It is now the only place in the world where stitchbirds can be seen in the wild. There are also many other exciting birds to look for, as well as giant earthworms (real giants – up to a metre long) and tuataras. Tuataras are extraordinary lizards with a distinctly prehistoric appearance. Until quite recently virtually nothing was known about these odd creatures, partly because they lead such sedentary lives that they were not considered to be

PEACE AND QUIET

The tuatara – a modern dinosaur?

likely candidates for exciting research. They are largely nocturnal but can occasionally be seen basking in the sunshine at their burrow entrance. Little Barrier Island is one of the few remaining islands where these animals survive. Permits to visit the island must be obtained in advance from the Hauraki Gulf Maritime Park Board, Department of Conservation, Auckland. For information on all the cruises available to other islands in the Hauraki Gulf Maritime park, visit the Cruise Centre which is at the back of Ferry Building in Auckland.

Rotorua

Visitors to Rotorua will find both a beautiful setting and plenty of wildlife interest. It lies at the heart of an area of thermal activity and the geysers and sulphurous smell testify to the forces at work beneath the ground. There are fine remnants of native forest here as well as lakes and wetlands full of birds. There are numerous spots around the shores of Lake Rotorua to look for water birds, as well as on the Blue and Green Lakes and Lake Rotomahana. In areas of dense marshy vegetation look for fernbirds, which are shy, behaving more like mice than birds.

Southeast of Rotorua lies **Whakarewarewa State Forest Park**, adjacent to Waimangu Road. The trees here are mainly introduced species. Eight marked trails allow visitors to explore the area. There is a Park Information Centre on Long Mile Road. North of Rotorua towards the Bay of Plenty lies the Rotoehu State Forest which contains remnants of native forest.

Tongariro National Park

Tongariro National Park, south of Lake Taupo in central North Island, was New Zealand's first national park. Highway 1 borders the eastern side of the park and there is a Visitor Centre on Highway 48. There is also access to the park from Ohakune. The park, which contains three active volcanoes – Mount Ruapehu, Mount Tongariro and Mount Ngauruhoe – is a popular skiing location, but despite the disturbance and associated development there is still plenty of wildlife.

Te Urewera National Park

Te Urewera National Park lies between Rotorua and Gisborne in north-central North Island. Together with adjacent Whirinaki Forest Park, it harbours some of the best remaining areas of native forest and bush left on North Island.

The scenery is stunning and the wildlife of the forest and Lake Waikaremoana is of considerable interest. There is a Visitor Centre at Aniwaniwa on Highway 38 where leaflets, advice on trails, and a display centre are available.

Cape Kidnappers Gannet Colony

Cape Kidnappers lies at the southern end of Hawke Bay on the east coast of North Island, and access along the promontory is by foot or on organised trips. Between August and January, large numbers of Australian gannets nest here, seemingly indifferent to the presence of their human onlookers.

Excellent views can be had of the birds and cameras are a 'must'.

Kowhai trees along Lake Taupo

Birds of Tongariro

Among the more natural areas of forest, look for birds such as riflemen, tomtits, New Zealand falcons, brown kiwis, parakeets, silvereyes and pied tits. In Pureora Forest Park, north of the national park, the forests harbour the rare and endangered kokako – a type of wattlebird. Around the shores of Lake Taupo, fernbirds and marsh crakes are found among the waterside vegetation and with luck visitors should see brown bitterns, spur-winged plovers and pukekos searching for water snails, insect larvae and fish. Open water species include New Zealand little grebe, black swans, New Zealand scaups and grey ducks.

Egmont National Park

Egmont National Park lies on the west coast of North Island near Cape Egmont. Established in 1900, it is dominated by the dormant, volcanic Mount Egmont. The forested slopes harbour many birds. The North Egmont Visitor Centre can be reached along Egmont Road from Egmont Village. Guided walks and a nature trail are available. The Dawson Falls Visitor Centre is reached from Kaponga and several walks of varying length are available. Heading south from the national park towards Wellington, the road passes Wanganui, where plenty of wetland birds can be found.

In and Around Wellington

Despite the fact that it is becoming a very modern city – normally a process incompatible with many forms of wildlife – there is still plenty to see in Wellington for those with an interest in natural history. The shores and harbours have coastal birds,

PEACE AND QUIET

nearby Kapiti Island has breeding sea birds and the Cook Strait offers some of the finest 'seawatching' in the whole country.

Within the city itself, parks and gardens are likely to hold starlings, house sparrows, blackbirds and chaffinches, all species introduced by settlers from Europe. However, on the outskirts of Wellington, more rural areas may have native scrub species such as New Zealand pigeons – sometimes seen feeding on berry bushes. Visit the Wellington Botanic Gardens (main gates on Glenmore Street) and Mount Victoria, from which forested walks lead back to the city. For a great variety of both coastal and scrub birds try to visit Kapiti Island. To reach it, head north on Route 1 to Paraparaumu. You must obtain a permit (free) in advance from the Department of Conservation, Wellington District Office. Many native species, including little spotted kiwis and various parakeets are frequently seen, as well as coastal birds such as gulls and

Little blue penguins

little blue penguins.

Crossing the Cook Strait between Wellington on the North Island and Picton on the South Island provides superb opportunities to observe the sea birds which regularly ply this narrow passage. Although the exact species present obviously vary according to the time of year and the weather, there will always be something of interest. Gulls, terns and Australian gannets are regular but there should also be less common visitors.

For the keen seawatcher, one journey may not be enough to do the birds justice, several crossings may have to be made.

Nelson

Waders, herons, wildfowl and gulls can be found on almost any suitable stretch of coast around Nelson but by far the best location in the area is on the long arm of Farewell Spit at the northern end of Golden Bay. The strandline is well worth exploring for shells, seaweeds, jellyfish floats, floating seeds and driftwood. From the southern point of Golden Bay – Separation Point – south can be found **Abel Tasman National Park**.

Established in 1942, the park protects fine areas of coast and also good areas of bush and forest. The national park headquarters are at 406 High Street, Motueka and 1 Commercial Street in Takaka. There are car parks along the coastal road from Takaka, from which short walks start, and another car park at Marahau.

Driving southeast from Nelson, the **Nelson Lakes National Park** can be reached. The mountainous terrain harbours scrub species, while wetland wildlife can be found around the shores of Lakes Rotoroa and Rotoiti.

In and Around Christchurch
Introduced species of birds are numerous in and around Christchurch, and within a comparatively short distance of the city visitors have the opportunity to explore native scrublands and can find excellent wetlands and colonies of breeding sea birds.
Within the city, visit the Botanic Gardens, South Hagley Park and North Hagley Park (all three lie close to the Avon River) while, further afield, Banks Peninsula lies to the southeast of Christchurch on Highway 75.

In and Around Dunedin
With planning and prior booking, visitors can see some excellent sea bird colonies in this southerly part of the South Island, and there is plenty to see within the city itself. Without doubt, the wildlife highlight of a stay in Dunedin is a visit to the Royal Albatross Colony at Taiaroa Head on the Otago Peninsula. Birds are present at the colony from mid-February until mid-September. The colony is fenced in and visits are strictly controlled to protect the birds from undue disturbance; bookings must be made in advance through the Dunedin Visitor Centre, 48 The Octagon.
Although masters of the air

A quizzical albatross

when flying over the sea, these immense birds are rather ungainly on land. Spotted shags also breed on the cliffs and there is a colony of yellow-eyed penguins near by on Taiaroa Head.
Visit the Botanic Gardens on George Street and the parks and gardens that comprise Town Belt to look for both native and introduced species of birds.

Arthur's Pass National Park
By driving northwest from Christchurch towards Greymouth, visitors cross the Southern Alps at Arthur's Pass, an area of outstanding scenery and the centre of Arthur's Pass National Park. There are numerous trails and nature walks, many of which start from

PEACE AND QUIET

Kiwis are rarely seen in the wild

Highway 73, and a Park Visitor Centre in Arthur's Pass. With many peaks within the park rising to over 5,000 feet (1,500m), the landscape is dramatic. In addition to admiring the views, explore the forest and scrub for native species.

Westland and Mount Cook National Parks

These two adjacent national parks lie on the divide of the Southern Alps in the west of South Island. With its towering peaks, cascading streams and alpine flowers, the scenery is stunning and the area is designated a World Heritage Area because of its beauty. Within the boundaries are the two highest peaks in New Zealand – Mount Cook at 12,350 feet (3,764m) and Mount Tasman at 11,474 feet (3,497m) – as well as many others over 10,000 feet (3,000m).
For Mount Cook, visitors generally stay at the Hermitage

Hotel in Mount Cook village, which has a good selection of wildlife in the vicinity. Wetland birds can be found around the shores of Lake Pukaki, while sooner or later a kea is likely to find you either just out of curiosity or in order to scrounge food. Introduced mammals such as red deer and chamois can also be seen, but their effect upon the native vegetation is generally less than welcome.
The Westland National Park Visitor Centre is in Franz Josef, and has information on trails and walks. The Mount Cook National Park headquarters are in Mount Cook village.

Mount Aspiring National Park and Lake Wanaka

Mount Aspiring National Park, New Zealand's second largest national park, lies further southwest along the chain of the Southern Alps from Mount Cook and Westland National Parks and contains 9,931-foot (3,027m) Mount Aspiring. The terrain includes alpine scrubland, thick forest and lake shores.
Information is available from the Visitor Centre, Ardmore Street in Wanaka. There are numerous trails and walks of varying length.

Fiordland National Park

Situated in the far southwest corner of South Island, this is the largest national park in New Zealand. The glacial scenery is stunning with deep fiords and U-shaped valleys carved by the action of ice, deep-blue lakes, cascading torrents and towering peaks.

Kea

One of New Zealand's native parrots, the kea is restricted to mountainous regions on the South Island. It has greenish-brown plumage with bluish wings and tail and a bright red underwing. The beak's upper mandible is long and downcurved. Keas feed on a variety of food, including fruit and insects. However, they will also take carrion and have even been accused – probably wrongly – of killing sheep. They nest in burrows or hollow tree trunks high in the mountains near the tree line. You do not need any special skills in order to see a kea; if there is one in your vicinity it will undoubtedly seek you out. They are very inquisitive, and very greedy, and they will regard you as a source of amusement or, better still, food.

The New Zealand blue duck

The wildlife of the area is also rich and varied: from scrub birds and water birds to exciting marine mammals and sea birds offshore.

Te Anau makes a good base from which to explore the national park: the park headquarters are here and near by is the shore of Lake Te Anau. The Bird Reserve here holds some of New Zealand's more threatened species.

There are numerous trails and paths within Fiordland National Park – information available at the park headquarters in Te Anau.

The coasts of Fiordland National Park are home to a wide range of sea birds as well as to marine mammals. **Milford Sound** is a good base from which to explore the coast, with many species of bird likely to be seen. Boat trips may yield sightings of Fiordland crested penguins, but more adventurous trips may be needed to see such creatures as dusky and Hector's dolphins, fur seals and sperm whales. The reason for the abundance of marine mammals and birds in these waters lies in the richness of the marine ecosystem and the lack of pollution.

Stewart Island

Separated from the mainland of South Island by the 18 mile (30km) Foveaux Strait, Stewart Island offers superb opportunities for visitors with an interest in natural history. Sea birds and coastal birds abound on the shores and seas that surround the island and the scrub and forest that remain still retain much of their original character.

PEACE AND QUIET

Crossing the Foveaux Strait by sea and not by air is a 'must' for anyone with an interest in sea birds. There can be few ferry crossings anywhere in the world that can rival the range and numbers of sea birds, and in particular albatrosses, that can be seen. Among the most frequently encountered are royal, Buller's, wandering and shy albatrosses, sooty shearwaters, diving petrels, giant petrels and the occasional penguin.

Introduced Species
Like many other parts of the world, New Zealand has its fair share of non-human colonists. Some were introduced by settlers either for food or to remind them of home, while others 'hitched a lift' on boats and among provisions. For example, many New Zealand towns and gardens have several elements in common with similar areas in Britain. Plants such as clovers, dandelions and ragwort grow in wayside areas, cabbage white butterflies take to the wing, house mice live alongside man and the birdlife includes species such as house sparrow, starling, blackbird, song thrush, chaffinch, goldfinch and greenfinch. Away from habitation, skylarks, yellowhammers and little owls can be found. Although the majority of introduced species simply add to the variety of New Zealand's wildlife, some have a less benign effect. Cats and stoats take a heavy toll on many bird species, and rabbits and red deer have caused

overgrazing.
Not all the new additions to New Zealand's wildlife have been due to man. In recent years, welcome swallows and white-faced herons have been natural colonists from Australia, and spur-winged plovers have also expanded their global range to include New Zealand. Even monarch butterflies have colonised in the past century.

Threatened Species
Because the wildlife of New Zealand evolved in an environment where ground mammals were absent – New Zealand's only native mammals are two species of bat – the animals, and especially the birds, did not have to cope with ground predators. That was, until man arrived on the scene, of course. Hunting and the introduction of predatory mammals and alien competitors, combined with habitat destruction and alteration, have wiped out some species and still threatens several of New Zealand's most interesting species.
Among the many species thought to have become extinct was an extraordinary bird called the takahe, a flightless and very large relative of moorhens. The last one was thought to have been killed in 1898, but some 50 years later a colony was discovered in the highlands near Lake Te Anau where they are now safeguarded and strictly protected. Unfortunately, the only takahes most visitors are likely to see are in the confines of Te Anau Bird Reserve.

FOOD AND DRINK

The cuisine of the Antipodes has taken an upturn in recent years, with imaginative use of local produce – meats, seafood and fruits. Top New Zealand chefs are now recognised internationally. Kiwi restaurants used not to be renowned for their presentation, but now offer their fare with flair, including a number of New Zealand delicacies – some being an acquired taste. Although typical 'kiwi' meals can be rich and full of calories, there has been a swing to healthier food, including vegetarian. There is now a wide variety of ethnic eateries as well – including Greek, Italian, Indian, Chinese, Mexican and, of course, Polynesian. But if you want authentic New Zealand food, look out for restaurants displaying the 'Taste of New Zealand' sign.

Where to Eat

There are full service restaurants, smorgasbord types (where one price covers a help-yourself meal of several courses), fast food outlets and takeaways of various kinds. The Cobb & Co chain of restaurants, found all over New Zealand, is good for family eating.

The international fast food chains of McDonalds, Kentucky Fried Chicken, and Pizza Hut are well represented throughout New Zealand. However fish and chips (French fries) remain a popular take-away; so too do Chinese and other Asian foods. Many public bars offer a limited menu of cooked meals – usually fried, with chips and salad. Small hot meat pies are also a popular take-away.

A Maori *hangi*, authentically food cooked on heated stones in an earth oven, is offered by some hotels (though sometimes they 'cheat' by pre-cooking the food). Rotorua is one of the best places for a *hangi*, where the natural earth heat has long been used by the Maori for their cooking. The food – lamb or pork, vegetables (often sweet potato) or seafood – is traditionally sandwiched between leaves, placed on the hot stones which have been sprinkled with water, then sealed in with earth to cook by steaming.

A 'licensed' restaurant is one that can sell glasses or bottles of liquor with meals at any time. Many restaurants have a BYO (bring your own wine) licence, but may charge a small

Hanging around for a *hangi*

FOOD AND DRINK

corkage fee for use of their glasses and service. Most restaurants listed in this book are fully licensed.

On the Menu

Starters

Kiwis favour soups in winter and salads in summer to start their meal, but both are always on the menu. Soups based on seafood are popular, especially those with *toheroa* (from the North Island) and *tuatua* (another local shellfish), and seafood chowder. Other usual starters include pâté or terrine, various vol-au-vent variations, and seafood in all its forms.

Seafood

New Zealand offers a wide choice of seafood as starters or main courses. In addition to soups, seafood cocktail (a salad with small prawns and other seafood with a dressing) is traditional. Specialist delicacies include Nelson scallops. Bluff (deep sea) oysters – from the far south of the South Island, caught in winter – and West Coast whitebait (a small finger-like fish usually served panfried in butter or in fritters), particularly from around Hokitika; also smoked salmon and smoked eel. Crayfish (rock lobster) is an expensive delicacy, but Kaikoura, north of Christchurch, is the place to eat it.

Popular fish include snapper, orange roughy, *tarakihi, hapuka*, flounder and, especially, John Dory and (in southern areas) blue cod. Salmon is reared in the south, but trout, a popular game fish, is not caught commercially and is not offered in restaurants. Some seafoods are seasonal.

Meat

As a sheep-rearing nation, the New Zealanders' traditional meat is roast lamb – or hogget, which is one-year-old lamb – served with a mint sauce or jelly. You can also get beef, chicken and pork, while venison is now farmed and available in some restaurants.

Vegetables

A wide variety of locally grown vegetables is available – potato, peas, beans and pumpkin in particular, but also lettuce, cabbage, cauliflower, carrots and leeks. In the South Island, parsnips and swedes are grown. Try roast *kumara* – a yellowish sweet potato.

Desserts

Fresh fruit and ice-cream are the usual dessert. The selection generally includes home-grown peaches, pears, apricots, strawberries and other varieties of berry fruit, and imported bananas or pineapples. Ice-cream, even plain or vanilla, is wholesome and full flavoured, while hokey-pokey, a kind of butterscotch, is popular. Pies, tarts, cream cakes and flans are frequently available, as is cheesecake. But the dessert New Zealand claims as its own (though Australians refute that) is the pavlova – a light fluffy meringue topped with freshly whipped cream and decorated with strawberries or kiwifruit (the prickly skinned fruit known as Chinese gooseberries until Kiwis exploited and marketed them). Tamarillos and passion-fruit are also used as toppings.

Cheeses
New Zealand makes its own fine cheeses of all kinds. Cheddars either mild or tasty, are most preferred, but Brie, Camembert, blue vein and others are available.

Drink
New Zealand grew up as a nation of beer drinkers, and still has a reasonably high per capita consumption. Bars and taverns are open daily until 23.00 hours or later.
The drinking age is 20 years, though 18- and 19-year-olds may drink in the company of someone older than 20. New Zealand brews a variety of draught and lager beers. Home produced white wines are winners, and are reasonably priced.
Chardonnays are internationally acclaimed, and Rhine Riesling and Müller Thurgau types are popular – and good. According to the experts, New Zealand red wine generally still has 'a little way to go'.
New Zealand makes and distils whisky, but most other spirits are imported. Sherries and ports are locally produced. Fresh milk and cream are readily available, always pasteurised, usually homogenised. Milk shakes and yoghurts are popular. Coca Cola and Pepsi, various aerated waters, and fruit juices are

Orange roughy, a fishy delicacy

available everywhere. Tap water is safe.
Tea and coffee are widely drunk: reasonably strong English-type tea and reasonably weak American-type coffee. A mid-morning and afternoon break for tea or coffee, or 'smoko', is cardinal.

Points to note:
- There is no tipping (unless service is exceptional).
- Check the menu to clarify whether GST tax of 12½ per cent is included or additional – it is usually included.
- 'Tea' can mean the evening meal or a cup of tea, while supper is an evening snack after dinner.
- Breakfast is rarely included in a hotel price.

SHOPPING

Although all cities have departmental stores, their numbers have declined in recent years. Specialist and boutique shops predominate. In larger cities, especially

SHOPPING

Auckland, large suburban shopping malls have halted, perhaps reversed, the growth of the downtown retail sector. Most shops are closed on Sundays. Although in Auckland and in most holiday resorts, some shops are open seven days a week.

Grocery shops and food supermarkets are sometimes open two or three nights a week. All over New Zealand 'dairies' are the corner convenience shops selling milk, bread, ice-cream, lollies and a range of foodstuffs and assorted other goods. Many dairies trade as mini-supermarkets, called 'superettes'. They are open daily, often with extended trading hours.

In some tourist areas – such as Queenstown – or at international airports, there may be longer trading hours for other shops too.

Village shopping in Auckland

For basic shop opening times see **Directory** page 122.

What to Buy

Sheepskins
As floor rugs, jackets, seat covers or single pelts for hangings, sheepskins are a popular visitor purchase. New Zealand has a sheep population of 65 million, so the range, quality and pricing of sheepskins is competitive.

Clothing
General clothing is not usually a bargain. However, items made in New Zealand are usually of good quality. Look for leather and suede from locally reared deer, which is good quality and good value.

Hand-knitted garments are another good buy, with some innovative designs. Look for sportswear, particularly 'Canterbury' brand, well known in New Zealand for colourful rugby shirts. Sports shoes, however are expensive. Outback Kiwis wear a thick felted-wool shirt called a 'Swanni', that may appeal.

Crafts
For its population, New Zealand has a high number of craftspeople working in every conceivable medium – wood, ceramics, metal, glass, fabrics. Auckland, Rotorua and Nelson are leading craft centres. Traditional Maori craftwork is a popular purchase. Native timbers are used for bowls, rulers and ornamental pieces. New Zealand nephrite jade, called greenstone, is made into

souvenirs. Hokitika is the main centre for greenstone working, but items are available elsewhere as well. Paua shell (abalone) is also used to decorate many souvenir items such as jewellery and teaspoons.

Cheaper Maori souvenirs – such as the ubiquitous *tiki* good luck emblem – are mass produced, but it is still possible to find good quality hand-made articles.

Other Specialities

New Zealand wines and cheeses make appealing souvenirs. You can even buy specially packed samples of the world-famous Bluff oysters, New Zealand venison or flavoured honeys and jams. There are also perfumes with the scent of native flowers. Records or cassettes of Maori singing are also pleasant souvenirs.

Duty Free

At airports and a few downtown locations there are duty free shops where liquor, tobacco and other products are sold free of tax to shoppers leaving the country. Although they may be selected and paid for in advance, such duty free goods cannot be collected until you are at the international airport on the day of departure. Auckland Airport also has an arrivals duty free shop, mainly for sales of liquor and tobacco, though of course purchases are still subject to the entry limitations (see **Customs Regulations** in the **Directory** page 116).

Tax

There is a Goods and Service Tax (GST) – a VAT-type consumption tax – of $12\frac{1}{2}$ per cent on all purchases; this is virtually always included in the price shown. There are no additional state or special taxes. Many goods may have a customs duty levied on them, but again these are always included in the shown price. All shoppers, including visitors, pay all the taxes included in a purchase price.

ACCOMMODATION

New Zealand has lots of good standard accommodation. The choice ranges from luxury hotels in the main cities and resorts to modest hotels, motels (New Zealand style), guesthouses, farms and private homes. You can even stay in a Maori meeting house. There are also campsites, National Park huts and youth hostels. Virtually anywhere in New Zealand you will find good, clean, acceptable accommodation – not always cheap, as the $12\frac{1}{2}$ per cent Goods and Service Tax (GST) bumps up the price.

A useful (free) publication listing most types of accommodation is the *New Zealand Where to Stay Guide*, produced jointly by the New Zealand Automobile Association and the New Zealand Tourism Board.

Hotels

Hotels in New Zealand are not graded. Respected international hotel groups such as Regent, Sheraton, Hyatt and Quality Inn

ACCOMMODATION

are represented in the main centres.

Some of New Zealand's most highly recommended hotels – on prime sites in top tourist areas – used to be in the government-owned THC (Tourist Hotel Corporation) chain. Most were sold to the Southern Pacific Hotel Corporation while this book was in preparation.

Prices in full service hotels start at around NZ$200 with higher prices in the main cities and resorts.

Throughout New Zealand you will find motor inns – not to be confused with motels. There is no fixed definition of a motor inn, but generally the term refers to reasonably new wings of accommodation with private facilities, all anchored to a central block housing reception, restaurant and a house bar. Generally there is plenty of (free) parking, and the price of NZ$100–$200 is less than for full service hotels.

In country areas, simple inexpensive accommodation is often available in pubs or taverns (note, however, that the word 'hotel' in the tavern's name does not necessarily mean that it is residential). Hotels do not usually include any meals in their pricing, though a few exclusive lodges offer an all-inclusive tariff.

Motels

Popular and reasonably inexpensive, the New Zealand motel is something other than a drive-in hotel. Motels consist of self-contained flats or apartments complete with cooking facilities, crockery, cutlery, dining and lounge furniture and usually a separate bedroom. Small motels may have only four or five units, but many have up to 30 or more. However, South Island motels are generally smaller than North Island ones. Many motels have a separate ironing room, games rooms and swimming pool or hot spa.

Prices range around NZ$50–$100 single/double. Motels are graded by the Automobile Association, and motor club members from overseas associations can get copies of the AA's accommodation guides. Many motels are owner operated, and some are affiliated with international booking chains such as Flag and Best Western.

Budget Accommodation

Most towns have a few guest houses and 'private' (meaning unlicensed for liquor) hotels. Although these sometimes lack private facilities, they often rate highly for atmosphere. There are YHA hostels in most towns featured in the gazetteer in this guide (see **Directory** page 124). There are also a number of private hostels, often older hotels, specialising in backpackers' accommodation. A brochure, *Backpackers Accommodation*, can be obtained from the New Zealand Tourism Board.

In national parks and conservation reserves there are 'huts' where trampers can stay overnight under shelter. For information on camping, see **Directory** page 116.

ACCOMMODATION/CULTURE AND ENTERTAINMENT

Meeting the People

Farm Stay and Home Stay are two special ways of meeting 'Kiwis'. With farm stays, visitors may participate in farming activities, and generally stay in the farm homestead or an adjacent cottage and dine with their hosts. Home stay, in either suburban or country locations offers similar opportunities. An association dealing with such stays is **Farmhouse and Country Homes Stays**, PO Box-31-250, Auckland 9 (tel: (09) 478 2843).

For a really different night's lodging you can stay on a *marae*, a Maori meeting place. You will take part in a greeting ceremony, enjoy a *hangi* dinner, and be entertained with Maori songs and dances. You have to join a group for a *marae* stay. For more information, contact New Zealand Board of Tourism.

A few other points:

● Check that GST (tax) is included in any quoted price.
● Most properties charge for extra people sharing, including children in some cases.
● There are no big seasonal differences in rates, but some properties may decline one-night bookings at holiday weekends or other peak times.
● Regardless of your choice of accommodation remember that the summer season and its shoulder months, from October through to April, coincide with the better weather, increased numbers of tourists, and the holidays of New Zealanders themselves. Most hotels are full in February and March; most

Graceful Maori poi *dancers*

motels are full in December and January. Booking ahead is advised, at least for these months and for school and public holidays.

CULTURE, ENTERTAINMENT AND NIGHTLIFE

Unique to New Zealand is the exciting culture of the Maori, but western-style orchestral music, opera, ballet and theatre is also well represented in the main cities. Outside town, the largely agricultural base of New Zealand's economy is reflected in shows of a peculiarly Kiwi type, with farming made into entertainment.

Maori Culture

Maori concerts are given nightly in Rotorua, and also frequently at venues in Auckland, Christchurch and Queenstown. The chants and actions of Maori warriors preparing for battle are remembered in the *haka*, while the women's *poi* dance (with flax balls on string) offers a gentler form of entertainment.

Maori singing is very harmonious and easy on the western ear – a combination of old lyrics presented in a European way. You should try to attend one such concert during your stay.

European Style Culture

Auckland, Wellington and Christchurch all have relatively new concert halls. There are five professional orchestras, and the Royal New Zealand Ballet.

Overseas artists and companies, pop musicians and other celebrities can often be seen, particularly in Auckland and Wellington. The latter city has a biennial Festival of the Arts of international standing (held on even-numbered years).

A & P Shows

Shows with a difference are the 'A & P Shows', distinctly agricultural and pastoral, held annually around many farming centres. Items with a farming bias, from tractors to prize pigs are on display. Hamilton, Christchurch and, especially, Rotorua and Queenstown, have daily tourist shows featuring farm animals, with displays from milking cows to shearing sheep. Attend one of these shows and be surprised at the professionalism and antics of the participants.

Parades

Teams of marching girls in colourful uniforms are a special and attractive New Zealand sight. Scottish heritage is readily shown in the many pipe bands through the country; there are also brass bands. Any parade has music and marchers galore. There are parades for Christmas, for farm shows, for rugby matches, and for provincial carnivals, such as the Alexandra Blossom Festival, or Hastings Easter Highland Games.

Nightlife

Nightlife in the swish form of Las Vegas or the Riviera does not exist in New Zealand. The country's first casino is scheduled to open in Christchurch in late 1994, followed by another in Auckland at a later stage. A few restaurants have a decorous pianist; so too do some hotel lounges. However, many taverns and public bars offer a trio of electric guitars and drums playing loud music. The main cities have discos, with recorded music, appealing to the younger set. Auckland and Wellington also have various strip clubs, gay bars, and massage parlours. All cities have cinemas, with latest release films.

WEATHER AND WHEN TO GO

Remember that 'down under' the seasons are reversed. In New Zealand summer is December, January and February, stretching into a summery autumn through to May, while winter starts in June, and spring in September. Remember, too, that the sun is in the northern sky. This means that it is warmer in the northern part of the country, though most northerly parts of the South Island can also get hot in summer. In general, the climate is sub-tropical in the north and temperate in the south, and there are no dramatic seasonal changes. The prevailing winds are westerly. The north-south mountain chain extending the length of the country, affects the movement of weather systems from west to east, making the west – particularly in the South Island – very wet. Most rain falls in winter – especially in the north. The south often receives snow, even at low altitudes. There is plenty of sunshine in general. Average daily sunshine hours are from seven to eight hours in summer, and four to five hours in winter. The north is generally very humid, with Auckland having high humidity and 'stickiness', while parts of the South Island are dry or have low humidity. Strong winds are a climatic feature, with Wellington having the reputation of the windiest place. Temperatures, indeed all weather, can be very local, with major differences 60 miles (100km) apart. In the mountains, storms can blow up quickly with gale-force winds and torrential rain sometimes causing rivers to flood.

When to Go

Most foreign visitors come to New Zealand in spring and summer. New Zealanders themselves take holiday breaks during the December-January period, so February-May and October-November are the most popular times for visitors.

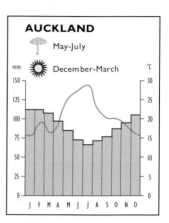

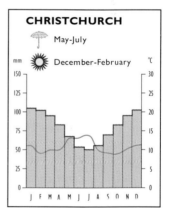

Skiers take to the hills in July through September.
Other times to avoid, when Kiwis also travel, are the holiday weekends of Easter and Labour Weekend (4th weekend of October).

What to Wear

Casual separates, which allow you to put on or take off items of clothing, are ideal for travelling in New Zealand. Sun glasses are essential. The sun can be deceptively, strong, and you would be advised to have a sun block with you in summer – especially in the north. The hole in the ozone layer is sometimes directly above New Zealand in November.

Carry a light raincoat in your baggage; if you are down south in winter, take a heavy coat.

HOW TO BE A LOCAL

New Zealanders are mostly of European stock – around 84 per cent – the majority of English or Scottish descent, though there are admixtures of Irish, Welsh, Dutch and other European blood.

About 9 per cent of the 3.35 million population claim Maori descent, but most of these would be of mixed Maori and Pakeha (white) descent. There are Pacific Islanders – mainly Polynesians (Auckland is the world's largest Polynesian community) – as well as Indians, Chinese, Indo-Chinese and Lebanese.

The national language is English, both spoken and read. The Maoris have their own language which is also an official language. Many place names are Maori, and there has been a resurgence of interest in recent years to ensure the survival of the Maori language. Many Kiwis do not know any language other than English, so visitors from non-English-speaking countries will have to brush up their English. Nevertheless, the relaxed lifestyle makes it easy to feel at home.

Maori carving, Rotorua

The Maoris

The Maoris were New Zealand's first human inhabitants, and before the arrival of Europeans they had no name for themselves as a people. 'Maori' means 'usual' or 'normal', which was how they differentiated themselves from the Pakeha, the white people who were to have such an effect on their lives.

The Europeans found a tribal society, regulated by a warrior code and given structure by a network of kinship links and traditions. Although most Maoris now live in towns as part of the urban society, efforts have been made in recent years to retain or revive the traditional basis of Maori life – with gatherings at *marae*, centred on elaborately carved meeting houses; with the teaching of Maoritanga (Maori culture) in schools; and with the establishment of nursery schools (Kohanga Reo) to teach young Maori children their own language. Visitors are welcomed at some *marae* and can even spend a night or two, taking part in ceremonies and listening to songs and stories. By learning something of the customs and traditions of the Maoris, a visitor can delve below the surface of the 'shows' they might see at tourist centres such as Rotorua. Today race relations in New Zealand are fairly good, although the loss of Maori lands which followed the signing of the 1840 Treaty of Waitangi is still a cause of some friction. However, the Maori and Pakeha are well integrated in the sense that one in 12 New Zealanders is half Maori and many more have some Maori blood.

Getting on with Kiwis

New Zealanders are considered to be very friendly people by visitors, though it is a characteristic possibly not fully realised by Kiwis themselves. They are rather reticent and you may have to draw them out by asking questions, but once you have made contact you will receive friendly, helpful assistance. You will be invited into people's homes and offered introductions to friends and relatives in other parts of the country.

Possibly because so many Kiwis have an English background, tourists and migrants from England can be the subject of friendly joking. English visitors should not, however, take offence at the term 'Pom', which is not meant to be abusive.

There is still a 'rugby, racing and beer' philosophy among some New Zealanders, evident in the high interest everywhere in sport of all kinds; but the liquor intake is now tempered by increasing concern about drinking and driving. Interest in sport is widespread, and if you want to know 'how to be a local', then keep up with the latest exploits of New Zealand sportspeople.

Acceptable Behaviour

Kiwis are a casual people. For men, a suit and tie is still worn in business circles, but an open-necked shirt and 'sports' jacket or blazer is more of a national costume. Female visitors will not look out of place in either a dress or slacks. Shorts are also acceptable casual attire for both men and women. Hats are not widely worn by either sex except when out in the sun. A minority of New Zealanders smoke. The habit is frowned upon by many, and smoking is restricted in a number of public places. Possession of drugs can lead to a fine or a year's imprisonment.

Topless or nude bathing is rare, and only done at the end of some more remote beaches. Gambling is a vice that is not discouraged. As keen followers of horse racing, Kiwis are also interested in placing bets. There is both on and off course betting – the latter through betting shops known as 'TABs' (because they are operated by the Totalisator Agency Board). However, individual bookmakers are forbidden. There is a national weekly

'Lotto' (drawn at 20.00 hours on Saturday – a big weekly event), and numerous local raffles. Casino gambling was illegal but that is now to change with the opening of a casino in Christchurch in late 1994.

There is no tipping in New Zealand. A friendly way to thank a Kiwi is to 'shout' (that is, pay for) a beer or other drink. The no tipping custom goes back to early New Zealand attitudes to tourism. It was felt that service to tourists entailed a servility that was unacceptable in an egalitarian society. As a result, service has been – and still is sometimes – less smooth and professional than some visitors might be accustomed to.

CHILDREN

Things to Do

There is plenty to interest younger visitors. For example, Auckland's **Kelly Tarlton's Underwater World** (page 20), **Rotorua's** geothermal activity (page 30), and **Queenstown's** jet boat rides (page 85) are adult attractions which children can also enjoy. Christchurch, Queenstown and Rotorua also have aerial gondolas – the latter with a popular toboggan or 'luge' track for a thrill-packed journey down from Mount Ngongotaha. The same towns, as well as several others, offer show **displays of farm animals** which might be of interest to children. Next to Rotorua's Agrodome attraction is a large **model railway**.

There are other model railways in Taupo and Napier. Vintage steam **trains** are operated by groups of enthusiasts throughout the country – especially at Auckland's **Glenbrook Vintage Railway** on summer Sundays, but also on many weekends in Wellington and Dunedin. And there is also the **Kingston Flyer**, south of Queenstown (see page 86).

There are a number of children's **recreational parks**. **Rainbow's End** in Auckland's southern suburbs is a family fun park, as is **Fantasyland** in Hastings.

Swimming is a popular pastime – not only at the beach. Most towns and suburbs have public swimming pools for family use, as do many motels.

Thermal pools are popular in Rotorua and elsewhere, which children will enjoy.

Special Arrangements

Age limits for children's prices vary but such prices usually apply to 12-year-olds and under (but sometimes up to 14 or 15). Some internal air fares have children's fares up to 14 years. There are also concessional fares on rail and bus services. Shows and cinemas also have children's prices.

In hotels and motels children are charged as adults at 12 years. Many better hotels do not charge for children sharing a room with adults. Many motels have children's play areas and equipment. Baby minding services are commonly available, but check before you book if this is important for you.

TIGHT BUDGET

New Zealand is not a cheap country if you are on a limited budget, but there are ways of making savings, with a little forethought and a little shopping around.

Travel

New Zealand, being so far from anywhere, is inevitably expensive to reach. Your travel agent is in the best position to find the cheapest and most convenient air fare deal for you. There is at time of writing, a joint 'Explore New Zealand Airpass' which allows travel on the flights of Air New Zealand and Mount Cook Airlines. These passes are only available for purchase overseas prior to arrival. Ansett New Zealand have special 'See NZ fares', available in connection with international travel; these can be purchased overseas or in New Zealand.

Within New Zealand, the Inter City network of rail, buses and inter island ferries offers passes for unlimited travel over 8, 15 and 22 days. Prices vary between high season (15 December to 31 January), and low season for other times. These passes are available to visitors on arrival. There is a separate Kiwi Coach Pass, allowing bus travel only for 7, 10, 15 and 25 days, which must be pre-purchased overseas. There are also bus passes for the Newman's coach lines in the North Island, and Mount Cook coaches in the South Island.

Rental cars can be expensive and there can be a big difference between companies' rates. However, it is a viable option for three or four persons travelling together. Prices tend to be cheaper with the 'unknown' firms – and for round trips. Remember that New Zealand consists of two islands, and ferrying cars over the connecting strait is not cheap. It is not illegal to hitchhike, but New Zealanders are not generous when it comes to offering free rides. Note that pedestrians are not allowed on motorways.

Accommodation

If you carry your home on your back, there is plenty of scope for camping in New Zealand (see **Camping** page 116). Many campgrounds, particularly those calling themselves holiday parks, offer cheap accommodation in basic huts, tourist flats or on-site vans. Department of Conservation huts with bunk beds, basic cooking facilities and a water supply, are an alternative for hikers. You pay in advance by buying tickets (NZ$4–12) from Department of Conservation offices.

For other budget accommodation suggestions, see **Accommodation** page 104 and **Directory**, page 124. There are various brochures available at gateway airports and at Visitor Information centres throughout the country that list budget accommodation, backpackers' hostels, and farm stay options. Notice boards in these hotels and lodges often list local deals, either advertised, or as useful tips left by previous travellers.

Eating

A good cooked breakfast ('grill') with eggs, bacon, sausage and tomatoes, though high in cholesterol, will last you until the evening meal, with just a little fruit for lunch. If you cannot stomach a full breakfast, then buy a take-away of hot pie or fish and chips for lunch, or bread and cheese from a dairy. Or you could have a snack in a tea room or café though this can turn out to be more expensive than you expect.

For dinner, a take-away is again the cheapest alternative. If you want a restaurant meal, seek out a BYO (bring your own) establishment, where you can take in a cheap bottle of wine and where the food is likely to be cheaper than in a licensed restaurant. For inexpensive refuelling, there is the Cobb & Co chain of pub restaurants, and fast food outlets like McDonalds and Pizza Hut.

Budget Tips

- Shop around for cheap air tickets.
- Think ahead – book your internal travel arrangements before you go.
- Out of town, stay in motor camps.
- In town, seek out the backpacker lodges.
- Buy take-away meals or picnics.
- If you like the occasional meal with wine, eat at a BYO restaurant.

SPECIAL EVENTS

Many special events in New Zealand are sports related – such as the yachting regatta in Auckland in January; Auckland's six-mile (10km) 'round the bays' fun-run in mid-March; the December motor race through Wellington's streets; and the November trotting (harness racing) festival in Christchurch. There are also numerous local and national sporting tournaments – especially tennis and cricket in summer, rugby and soccer in winter.

Arts festivals are held in the main cities – the principal one being Wellington's biennial autumn attraction.

As in the UK, New Zealand children light fireworks on 5 November to celebrate Guy Fawkes's attempt to blow up the British Parliament in 1605 - though most Kiwi kids don't know much about that: it's just a fun occasion.

There are also local festivals, such as:

March – Masterton Golden Shears Sheep Shearing competition.

April – Arrowtown Autumn Festival; New Zealand Easter Show, Auckland.

Easter – Hastings Highland Games.

June – Hamilton's National Agriculture Field Days.

September – Alexandra Blossom Festival.

October – New Plymouth Rhododendron Festival.

Christmas/New Year – Caroline Bay Christmas Carnival in Timaru.

SPORT

Surrounded by New Zealand's wonderful scenery, it is no wonder that Kiwis are an outdoor, sports-loving people. For its size New Zealand has an impressive international reputation in the sporting field.

Spectator Sports

Horse-racing heads the list here. There are at least two or three horse-racing or trotting (harness racing) meetings on any Saturday – with more in summer. Such meetings are held throughout New Zealand, but especially in Auckland, Christchurch and Wellington. **Football** watching – and playing – is a popular winter pastime. Rugby predominates and the 'All Blacks' team is world renowned. Provincial and local games are well supported. Soccer is also popular; rugby league to a lesser extent. **Cricket** is a summer sport in New Zealand. Both three-day matches and one-day games attract a large following. There are many **athletics meetings**.

Participant Sports

Golf is very popular. All cities and towns have at least one golf course – nearly 400 in all. Particular courses noted for their appeal include Waitangi in the Bay of Islands, The Grange, Titirangi, and Middlemore in Auckland, Wairakei International near Taupo, Paraparaumu Beach, Hutt, and Wellington in Wellington, Russley and Shirley in Christchurch, Balmacewan and

St Kilda in Dunedin, and Millbrook Resort in Queenstown.

There are many **tennis** clubs throughout New Zealand; also many **bowling** clubs, both indoor and lawn. **Squash** and **badminton** courts, fitness centres and aerobic classes are everywhere.

The most popular female participant sport is **netball** – played in winter.

Boating is a favourite Kiwi pastime. You can go cruising in the harbour and gulf of Auckland, the Bay of Islands, the Marlborough Sounds, the lakes of Rotorua, or the lakes and fiords of the south. All tourist boats are modern launches, hydrofoils or big catamarans. You can hire your own yacht for cruising in Auckland or the Bay of Islands. New Zealand is a fisherman's paradise. The most common **fishing** is just casting a line over the side of a boat to see what is biting. On inland lakes and rivers trout fishing is

You could fall for bungy jumping

SPORT

'To the ocean now I fly'

popular – year round on the Rotorua, Taupo and Southern Lakes. Trout fishing is probably best in summer. A licence, at minimal cost, can be readily purchased. Salmon fishing is also available on some South Island rivers in summer. Guided line fishing is available from charter boats all around the country; there is big game fishing from Russell in the Bay of Islands, also from Tauranga. **Skiing** is popular in winter. National Park and Ohakune are the North Island centres for skiing (June to October). In the South Island, Queenstown and Mount Hutt are the leaders, but there are many other fields.

Adventure Sports

New Zealand has plenty of outdoor adventure opportunities. **Jet boating** at speed on South Island rivers, mainly at Queenstown, is a thrilling experience. **Rafting** on white water is popular especially in areas near Tauranga, Whakatane and Queenstown. You can **canoe**, in summer, for five days down through the wilderness of the Wanganui River.

Underwater **diving** is best along the east coast north from Tauranga and Auckland. A new thrill is **black water rafting** – floating through underground caves. **Caving** – without water – is available in the Waitomo and Nelson areas. **Mountaineering** is possible in the southern Alps, particularly at Mount Cook, Wanaka and Fox Glacier. **Hunting**, preferably with a guide, is available year round in many places throughout both islands.

Hiking and **tramping** are popular for locals and visitors. There are hundreds of walks and tracks of varying standards throughout national parks, forest reserves and along coastlines. Auckland's Waitakere Ranges provides bush tracks close to New Zealand's largest city. The Coromandel Peninsula near Thames and the plateau country of Rotorua and Taupo provide more opportunities. In the South the Nelson area offers bush and beach tramps through the Abel Tasman National Park and the Heaphy Track; while the guided walks of Fiordland – the Milford, Hollyford, Routeburn and Greenstone – give three or four days of scenic mountain splendour. Advance bookings are essential for guided walks. New Zealand's latest thrill adventure is **bungy jumping**: willing participants are tied around the ankles with an elastic rope and dive from certain bridges. Backpackers, usually careful with their money, come from all parts of the world to pay for a go!

DIRECTORY

Contents

Arriving
Camping
Crime
Customs Regulations
Disabled
Driving
Electricity
Embassies and
    Consulates
Emergency
    Telephone
    Numbers

Entertainment
    Information
Health
Holidays
Lost Property
Media
Money Matters
Opening Times
Personal Safety
Pharmacies
Places of Worship
Police

Post Office
Public Transport
Senior Citizens
Student and Youth
    Travel
Telephones
Time
Tipping
Toilets
Tourist Offices
Travel Agencies

Arriving

By Air

Most visitors arrive by air, through the three international airports of Auckland, Wellington and Christchurch. Auckland is the largest gateway, with over 20 airlines. It is possible to fly direct to Auckland from UK and Europe and from US (cheapest from the West Coast).

Air New Zealand is the national airline. Head office: Air New Zealand House, 1 Queen Street, Auckland 1 (tel: (09) 366 2400). There is a bank and exchange facilities, restaurants and shops at Auckland airport. Wellington and Christchurch airports have similar facilities.

There are regular coach services from each airport to the downtown area. Shuttle vans provide a service to all suburbs. Taxis and rental cars are also available.

An international departure tax is payable by all passengers 5 years and over.

By Sea

Visitors arriving by sea inevitably dock in Auckland, where the Passenger Shipping Terminal is only one short block from the foot of the main street.

Entry Formalities

A passport, with at least three months' validity beyond the intended stay, is required by visitors. Australian citizens do not need a visa; nor for a period of up to six months (extension up to one year for tourists), do British citizens who have the right of permanent residence in the UK. Most citizens of western Europe, including Ireland, France, Germany, Netherlands and Italy, also Japan, Singapore, US and Canada can enter on tourist visits for up to three months without visas. However, all tourists, business travellers and others should recheck entry documentation in advance of their arrival.

Visitors must have onward or return tickets to a country they are permitted to enter, and have sufficient funds to maintain themselves while in New

DIRECTORY

Zealand. Every visitor must complete an arrival card.

Camping

Generally, you may camp anywhere on public ground. Whereas campgrounds come in all standards, most provide central communal toilets and shower blocks, kitchen and laundry rooms, and often a TV or games room. Charges for a tent site start at about NZ $8 per night per adult; camp sites for two with power for motorhomes start at about NZ $9 per night per adult. Many campgrounds also offer cabins, ranging from huts with bunks, to tourist flats, to motels. Bedding is not usually supplied but can sometimes be hired.

During the months of December and January it is recommended to book ahead for camp site reservations, but this is probably not necessary at other times.

The *AA Accommodation Guide* provides a graded list of camp-sites.

Camp and Cabin Association, PO Box 394, Paraparaumu (tel: (04) 298 3283). (Write for information only).

Chemists
see **Pharmacies**

Crime

Despite the apparently easy-going way of life, tourists should still be vigilant. Crime does exist and is on the increase. A few precautions should therefore be taken. There are no districts of New Zealand more dangerous than others, but the dark back streets of downtown areas should be avoided. Do not walk alone in lonely streets or country areas. Even women in twos should avoid dark streets, quiet buildings and car parks at night-time. Avoid flaunting leather or suede jackets, expensive fashion boots, jewellery or purses unnecessarily. Avoid flashing wallets, passports, credit cards or room keys in public bars. Do not leave cars unlocked, and do not leave valuable items on view in cars. If hitch-hiking, it is advisable to travel with a companion. Most hotels provide safes or safety deposit boxes to guard valuables. Hand room keys to the front desk when leaving your hotel for a while.

Customs Regulations

As an island nation, New Zealand has remained largely free of most of the major animal and plant diseases and pests. Consequently, some overseas flights will be subject to a cabin spraying, which is harmless for humans. Arriving passengers must also complete a declaration certifying whether foodstuffs, animal products or plant matter are in their baggage.

Firearms must be declared, and some weapons are prohibited. Narcotic drugs are generally prohibited, though a small supply can be carried for medical reasons if suitably identified and certified by a doctor's certificate or prescription. There are severe penalties for carrying any illegal drugs.

Travellers may bring in their own personal effects provided that such items are for personal use, and are exported with the traveller on departure. Passengers 17 years of age and over may bring in 200 cigarettes, 50 cigars, or 250 grams of tobacco. They may also bring in 4.5 litres of wine, and one bottle of up to 1.125 litres of spirits or liquour. Other 'dutiable goods' to the value of NZ $700 may be exempted from customs duty and GST (Goods and Service Tax).

Disabled

Facilities for the disabled are available at airports, and at many public amenities such as theatres, shopping malls, and toilets. Most newer accommodation houses have one or more units for the physically disabled. Official accommodation guides state whether hotels, etc, have facilities for the disabled. For information on facilities throughout New Zealand, write to **The Disability Resource Centre**, PO Box 24–042, Royal Oak, Auckland.

Driving

New Zealand's first rule of the road is keep left. Road standards are generally good, but variable. Auckland and Wellington have main outlets of motorway/freeway standard from the city centres to outer suburbs (no cyclists or pedestrians are allowed). Most rural and inter-city roads are tar-sealed, with at least one lane in each direction.

However, some country roads are unsealed, with a 'metalled' surface of gravel and the danger of skidding and flying stones. Watch for single-lane bridges on some rural roads.

Breakdowns and Accidents

In the event of vehicle breakdown there are plenty of motor garages and service stations throughout the country – although mechanical assistance may be limited at weekends. If your vehicle is rented, the operator will advise instructions in the event of a breakdown.

If you have an accident in a rental vehicle, you should let the operator know immediately. Obtain the name, address and insurance company of the owners of any other vehicles involved. If there are any personal injuries in a vehicle accident, the police must be advised

Car Rental

You must be at least 21 years of age to rent a car.

International Driver's Licences are recognised, though drivers from Australia, UK, US and Canada, may drive on their own licences if valid for up to twelve months.

Third party personal insurance is compulsory. Vehicle insurance is sold with car rental, though there may still be a franchise or excess amount that hirers pay in the event of damage. Insurance excludes some roads considered hazardous – read the small print.

If you are visiting both islands, check whether you are obliged

DIRECTORY

to take your rental car with you on the inter-island ferry between Wellington and Picton, or whether you can change over vehicles.

For motorhomes, the major rental operators are Newmans, Mount Cook, and Maui. Vehicles range from two-berth pop-top camper vans to big five- or six-berth units. Rental rates generally include unlimited distance, but may require you to add insurance and tax.

Rates are dearest in December and January, and much cheaper in winter. Most campgrounds provide electrical connections for motorhomes. Depots are situated at Auckland and Christchurch, which usually means that you take, and pay for, any inter-island crossing required.

The major car rental firms are represented, as well as a number of smaller ones. Some head office addresses:

Avis, Building 4, Central Park, 666 Great South Road, Penrose, Auckland.

Hertz, 48 Lichfield Street, Christchurch.

Endless scenery and the open road

Budget, 83 Beach Road, Auckland central.

Chauffeur-driven Cars
Chauffeur-driven cars are available for touring, short excursions or airport transfers. Advance booking is usually essential. Alternatively, taxi companies frequently have personnel able to drive for short duration tours of up to a few days.

Fuel
Petrol comes in two grades: super (96 octane), and partially unleaded (91 octane). Diesel is also available. LPG (liquified petroleum gas) and CNG (compressed natural gas) are also available (the latter not in the South Island). Be prepared for service stations to be few and far between – and possibly closed when you find one, although most major centres have 24-hour ones.

Motoring Organisations
The Automobile Association in New Zealand is well represented throughout the country, and members of affiliated overseas motor clubs obtain reciprocal service on presentation of their current membership card.

New Zealand Automobile Association, 99 Albert Street, Auckland.

Speed Limits
Distances and speed are measured in metric. Accordingly the speed limit in 'built up areas', as signposted, is 50kph (31mph), while on the 'open road' it is 100kph (62mph). Most road signs follow the international system.

Traffic Law

Traffic law is controlled and enforced by police officers. It is an offence to drive a motor vehicle with a blood/alcohol level exceeding 80 milligrams of alcohol per 100 millilitres of blood. Roadside tests and blood samples may be taken at random from any driver. It is mandatory for drivers and passengers to wear seat belts as fitted.

Electricity

Consumer supply voltage in New Zealand is 230 volts AC. The plugs have three flat pins. Most hotels and many motels have built-in converters accepting 110-volt American-style plugs; however, they are usually for shavers only. You may therefore require an adaptor plug, but you should also check that any electrical appliance you have is able to operate on 230 volts or is connected to a voltage transformer.

Embassies and Consulates

Wellington is the main location for most embassies, but UK, US, Canada and Australia are also represented by consulates in Auckland.

Australian High Commission, 72–78 Hobson Street, Thorndon, Wellington (tel: (04) 473 6411)
British High Commission, 44 Hill Street, Wellington (tel: (04) 472 6049)
Canadian High Commission, 61 Molesworth Street, Wellington (tel: (04) 473 9577)
US Embassy, 29 Fitzherbert Terrace, Thorndon, Wellington (tel: (04) 472 2068)

Consulates in Auckland

Australian Consulate General, Union House, 32–38 Quay Street (tel: (09) 303 2429)
British Consulate General, Fay Richwhite Building, 151 Queen Street (tel: (09) 303 2973)
Canadian Consulate, Princes Court Building, 2 Princes Street (tel: (09) 309 8518)
US Consulate General, General Building, corner of Shortland and O'Connell Streets (tel: (09) 303 2724).

New Zealand Embassies Abroad

Australia: NZ High Commission, Commonwealth Avenue, Canberra ACT 2600 (tel: (06) 270 4211)
Canada: NZ High Commission, Metropolitan House, Suite 801, 99 Bank Street, Ottawa, Ont KIP 6G3 (tel: (613) 238 5991)
UK: NZ High Commission, New Zealand House, The Haymarket, London SW1Y 4TQ (tel: (071) 930 8422)
US: NZ Embassy, 37 Observatory Circle NW, Washington DC 20008 (tel. (202) 328 4848).
There are also consulates in Los Angeles and San Francisco.

Emergency Telephone Numbers

The nationally recognised emergency telephone number is 111. This puts you in contact with Police, Fire, or Ambulance – the service you are needing should form the first part of your call. Full instructions on emergency telephoning can be found in the front of telephone directories or beside public telephones.

DIRECTORY

Entertainment Information

Most tourist areas have a local 'What's On' brochure available in accommodation houses and information centres. In addition, amusements and sports events are featured in newspapers. In Auckland look for a complimentary copy of the *Auckland Tourist Times*. The Rotorua area is included in a similar tabloid, *Thermal Air*, covering the 'Tourist Diamond' of the Bay of Plenty and Taupo. Down Queenstown way another tabloid, *Mountain Scene*, covers the Southern Lakes area (see also **Media** – under **Radio**).

Entry Formalities

see **Arriving**

Health

No special health or vaccination certificates are needed to enter New Zealand. However, if within three weeks of arrival you develop any general illnesses, fevers, or rashes, you should consult a doctor and tell him where you have travelled from. Hotels and motels have arrangements with duty doctors and local medical services. Some medical services are subsidised for visitors from Australia and UK, because of reciprocal health care schemes. However, all visitors are strongly recommended to arrange medical insurance cover in advance of their trip. If a visitor to New Zealand suffers a personal injury, he or she is entitled to claim from the 'Accident Compensation' system, irrespective of fault. Benefits available include some medical and hospital expenses. It is therefore not possible to sue for damages for personal injury or death by accident in New Zealand. Concern about Aids is increasing, although the number of cases is still relatively low.

Holidays

Christmas Day (25 December). **Good Friday** (at Easter weekend), and **Anzac Day** (25 April) – the memorial day for the dead of two world wars – are three days when most shops and tourist attractions will be closed.

Other Public Holidays

New Year (1 and 2 January)
Waitangi (New Zealand) Day (6 February)
Easter Monday
Queen's Birthday (first Monday in June)
Labour Day (fourth Monday in October)
These are national public holidays with most shops closed but many tourist amenities open. There are also regional holidays celebrating the founding of the provinces.

Lost Property

Report any serious loss of property to the police. Should you later be making an insurance claim you may be required to submit proof of your police reporting. For lost passports inform the nearest Embassy or Consulate of the issuing country (see under **Embassies and Consulates**). Lost credit cards or travellers' cheques should be reported to the issuing company.

Media

Newspapers and Magazines
New Zealand's largest circulation newspaper is the Auckland morning daily (not Sundays), *The New Zealand Herald*, but all the main cities produce daily morning editions. Local and international magazines are widely available. Magazines such as *Time* and *Newsweek* are current, but many overseas hobby and other publications arrive by sea mail a few weeks or months late.

Radio
New Zealand's four national radio networks include two non-commercial programmes: the National Programme on the AM band, specialising in news, talks and information; and the Concert Programme (on FM stereo) broadcasting classical music. The two commercial stations broadcast popular music. There are also local commercial stations. Broadcasting is in English with the occasional programme in the Maori language.
Tourist Information FM (88·2 MHz) broadcasts 24-hour information on New Zealand's history and culture, plus local attractions.

Television
There are three TV channels, broadcasting news and popular shows and documentaries from the UK, the US and Australia – as well as local productions.

Money Matters
New Zealand currency is

Rugby is a national passion

decimal-based and divided into dollars and cents. The New Zealand dollar is not tied to any other currency. Generally its value is around 75–80 per cent of an Australian dollar, 50 per cent of a US dollar, or 35 per cent of a pound sterling.
The coins now in circulation are in denominations of 5, 10, 20 and 50 cents and one and two dollars. Notes are in denominations of 5, 10, 20, 50 and 100 dollars.
Trading banks are open 09.30–16.30hrs Monday to Friday, except public holidays. There are plenty of bank branches in all towns. Thomas Cook and American Express, and some banks, operate Change Bureaux. Banks at international airports are open for all international flights. Credit cards widely accepted include Access/Mastercard, Visa, Diners Club and American Express. They may be used for most amenities and purchases. There is no restriction on the amount of foreign or New Zealand currency that may be brought into or taken out of the country.

DIRECTORY

Opening Times

Shops
Shops and stores generally open 09.00–17.30hrs Monday through Thursday. Late opening, until 21.00hrs, is usually on Friday, though some areas have late night shopping on Thursday. Saturday opening is usually 09.00–12.00 or 09.00–16.00hrs. Some shops now open on Sundays (10.00–14.00hrs). In tourist areas and resorts, shops are invariably open in the evening and on Sundays.
Banks see **Money Matters.**

Personal Safety
The usual commonsense precautions should be taken to prevent any personal injury, such as avoiding walking alone in dark areas of towns.
When setting off on a long walk into the bush or mountain country, you should always: dress sensibly; make sure you have good maps; take supplies of food and drink; and tell someone what your plans are. Earthquakes are a real hazard. You can find emergency advice on the back page of telephone directories.
New Zealand's wildlife presents few dangers to human beings. However, it should be noted that there exists one poisonous spider, the very rare katipo spider, which occurs on beaches but which you are unlikely to encounter. Sandflies, however, are prevalent in some areas – notably Milford Sound – and wasps are a nuisance in beech forests, notably around Nelson. Both can be unpleasant.

Take a good insect repellent. See also **Crime**.

Pharmacies
All cities, suburbs and towns have pharmacies. Generally they keep the same opening hours as other shops, but in larger towns and suburbs there will be an 'Urgent Dispensary' open for limited times out of hours (ask your hotel or motel staff). Pharmacies stock a wide range of products, including consumer drugs, health and beauty items, first aid and birth control products, and some photographic products.

Place of Worship
Most New Zealanders are Christian with the major denominations being Church of England (Anglican), Presbyterian, and Roman Catholic. Baptists and Methodists are also widespread and other sects are represented. Churches of the main denominations are located in most towns, and cities. Places of worship of minor Christian sects, as well as synogogues and mosques, may be found in the larger cities.
Newspapers carry notices regarding church services, and hotels and motels will assist with information regarding locations and times.

Police
There is an efficient police force modelled on the British system. Police do not carry arms.
In emergency, dial 111 for police.

Post Office

The logo for NZ Post Limited is a stylized envelope. It is a reasonably efficient organisation, and both domestic and overseas mail is handled promptly. Distinguish between Standard Post (usually surface mail) and dearer Fastpost (usually airmail) when posting letters and parcels.

Poste restante collection service is available from counters at principal post offices in each city.

Most post offices are open 09.00–17.00hrs Monday to Friday (in main cities until 19.00hrs and Saturday mornings).

Many shops sell stamps, and in rural areas, general stores often supply postal services.

NZ Post Chief Post Office is at Queen Elizabeth II Square, Lower Queen Street, Auckland.

Public Transport

Air

Three airlines, **Air New Zealand, Mount Cook Airlines** and **Ansett New Zealand**, fly the principal air routes with jet aircraft within the country.

They link Auckland, Wellington, Christchurch and Dunedin; altogether over 30 destinations. Ansett and Mount Cook Airlines both fly the tourist route from Rotorua to Christchurch and Queenstown. Smaller commuter airlines link a number of other centres. Air New Zealand and Mount Cook Airways market a joint 'Explore New Zealand Airpass' for visitors. The pass must be bought before you come to New Zealand, but can be open-dated.

Addresses:
Air New Zealand, see **Arriving**
Ansett NZ, 75 Queen Street, Auckland (tel: (09) 302 2146)
Mount Cook Airline, 47 Riccarton Road, Christchurch (tel: (03) 348 2099)

Rail

The New Zealand railways system, called **NZ Rail**, operates long distance trains: two between Auckland and Wellington; links to Tauranga and Rotorua; a daily train from Wellington to Hastings and Napier; a daily train linking Christchurch with the inter-island terminal at Picton; the scenic 'Tranz-Alpine Express' train from Christchurch to Greymouth; and the 'Southerner', south from Christchurch to Dunedin and Invercargill.

There are various InterCity flexible passes allowing unlimited travel at a fixed price for so many days. You can travel 8 days out of 14, 15 days out of 22, or 22 days out of a month. Some Travelpasses also allow travel on ferries operated by the railways.

NZ Rail, Travel Centre, Beach Road, Auckland.

Buses and Coach Tours

The InterCity bus network covers much of the country, including many of the tourist areas. **Newmans Coachline**, in the North Island operate on all major routes such as Auckland to New Plymouth, Napier to Wellington, and

DIRECTORY

Craftshops are interesting and worth investigating

Nelson to Christchurch. **Mount Cook Line** operate all the major South Island routes. A number of companies operate a frequent series of inclusive coach tours, combining transport, accommodation and most meals. The South Island has various 6–11-day tour options; and there are 3–4-day connecting tours in the North Island.
Newmans Coachline, PO Box 37248, Auckland.

Ferries
The inter-island ferry service is operated by the Railways Corporation. It is a roll-on roll-off service carrying passengers, motor vehicles and railway wagons. There are four return sailings from Wellington to Picton each day, taking just over 3¼ hours each way.
Passengers can usually be accommodated at short notice, but advance bookings for motor vehicles are essential in December and January.
The Inter-islander, NZ Rail Ltd, Private Bay, Wellington.

Senior Citizens
There are no special hazards of New Zealand travel, transport, terrain or climate that would effect older tourists who are in reasonable health. NZ Rail have a 'Golden Age Saver' with a 30 per cent discount on all their services on the standard adult fare for those over 60. You must have some proof of your age.

Student and Youth Travel
There is a Youth Hostel Association affiliated with the International Youth Hostel Federation. The YHA Head Office address is PO Box 436, Christchurch, and you can visit them at 28 Worcester Street, Christchurch (tel: (03) 379 9970). The Auckland office is at Australia House, 36 Customs Street East (PO Box 1687) (tel: (09) 379 4224)
There are YMCA and YWCA Hostels in the larger cities, offering basic accommodation and often breakfast and dinner to travellers.
Student Travel Services in New Zealand is at 233 Cuba Street, Wellington. They also have offices at the universities in Auckland, Christchurch, Dunedin, Hamilton and Palmerston North. These offices

have information on a wide range of student travel concessions and issue International Student Identity Cards.

NZ Rail has a 30 per cent concession scheme for students on their rail, coach and ferry services.

Air New Zealand and Ansett has a space-available discount (50 per cent) on internal air flights for holders of International Student Identity Cards. YHA members receive discounts on Newmans and Mount Cook Bus Lines.

Telephones

Telecom operate the public phone service in New Zealand. For Directory Enquiries dial 018.

To telephone New Zealand from abroad, dial the country access code (0011 from Australia, 010 from the UK, 011 from the US and Canada and 16 from the Irish Republic), then 64 followed by the area code (omitting any initial '0') and the subscriber number. Internal toll calls require a '0' access code followed by the STD code. International calls require the '00' access code, followed by the required country code, area code, and local number. Country codes are: for Australia 61, UK 44, US and Canada 1, Irish Republic 353. New Zealand's country code is 64.

Most public callboxes use phone cards, available from Telecom offices and some shops.

Your hotel or motel will have instructions on how toll calls should be placed in their establishments (but remember telephone calls made from these establishments are usually more expensive). Inland toll calls and some overseas calls are cheaper at night.

Time

New Zealand's closeness to the International Date Line makes it one of the first countries in the world to see each new day. Local time is 12 hours ahead of Greenwich Mean Time (GMT), 2-4 hours ahead of Australia, 17-22 hours ahead of the US and Canada. In summer (October to March), local clock time is advanced one hour.

Tipping

Tipping is not required. Service charges are not added to hotel bills, but remember that Goods and Service Tax (GST) of 12½ per cent is collected on all items. Usually this is included in the published price though some restaurants do not always show it. Do not confuse the tax with a tip.

Toilets

Public conveniences are located in the downtown areas of all towns and in many shopping malls or departmental stores. Some petrol stations also have toilets.

Tourist Offices

The New Zealand Tourism Board's head office is in Wellington (PO Box 95) (tel: (04) 472 8860).
Addresses for overseas tourist

offices are as follows:

Australia: Prudential Finance House, 84 Pitt Street, Sydney, NSW 2000; or GPO 614, NSW 2001 (tel: (02) 231 1322)
UK: New Zealand House, Haymarket, London SW1Y 4TQ (tel: (071) 973 0360)
US: 501 Santa Monica Boulevard, Suite 300, Santa Monica, CA 90401 (tel: (800) 388 5494).

Within New Zealand there is a network of Visitor Information Centres. The addresses of many of these are shown in each regional section of this book.

Travel Agents

There are over 500 travel outlets in New Zealand, although not all promote internal travel.

Air New Zealand have a number of travel offices booking air travel and accommodation. The Automobile Association in New Zealand operates a network of outlets known as **AA Travel**, with offices in all major cities handling accommodation and travel reservations.

LANGUAGE

The common language of New Zealand is English. In the written language British spelling is followed, rather than American usage. There is little difference in pronunciation from one part of the country to another, except that in the South you

may notice a touch of Scottish accent.

There have been attempts to retain and revive the Maori language in case it should disappear. However, the only examples of it that visitors are likely to encounter are in place names. Maori place names are basic descriptions, though some refer to deeds or events that have occurred in that place, either in reality or legend. A list with the meanings of a few words found in place names is given below.

Pronunciation is phonetic. Each syllable is spoken and there is an equal stress on each.

Aotearoa Land of the Long White Cloud (a descriptive name for New Zealand)
ara path
awa river, valley
hau wind, air
hua fruit, berry
huka cold
kai food, to eat
mana prestige, authority
manga stream
paku small
papa flat
puke hill
raki north
roa long
roto lake
rua hole, pit, two
runga top
tahu light
tai sea
tane male person
tapu sacred
tara peak
te the
utu revenge
wai water

INDEX

Page numbers in *italics*
refer to illustrations

accommodation 103–5,
  111–12
  (see also individual
  locations)
airports and air
  services 111, 115, 123
Akaroa 57
Alexandra 77–8
Aratiatia Rapids 33
Arrowtown 85
Arthur's Pass National
  Park 60, 95–6
Auckland 4, 6, 13–24,
  16, 90–1, *102*
Avon River 54, *54*

Banks Peninsula 56–7
Bay of Islands 13, *25*,
  25–8
Blenheim 67
Bluff 78, *78*
budget tips 111–12
buses 123–4

Cable Car 39
camping 116
Cape Foulwind 68
Cape Kidnappers 93
Cape Reinga 28, *29*
car rental 111, 117–18
casinos 106
chemists 122
children's
  entertainment 110
Christchurch 53–9, *55*,
  95
City Art Gallery
  (Auckland) 16
climate 8, 106–7
Coromandel Peninsula
  13, *34–5*, 35
Coronet Peak 85
countryside and
  wildlife 90–8
cultural events 105–6
currency 121
customs regulations
  116–17

disabled travellers 117
Domain and Museum
  17–18
dress 107–8

driving 117–19
Dunedin 69–77, *71*, 95

Eastwoodhill
  Arboretum 48
Egmont National Park
  93
embassies and
  consulates 119
emergencies 119
entertainment and
  nightlife 105 6, 120
  (see also individual
  locations)
Expo Pavilion of New
  Zealand 17

ferries 124
Ferrymead Historic
  Park 55
festivals and events 112
Fiordland National Park
  69, 80, 96–7
food and drink 99–101,
  112
Fox and Franz Josef
  Glaciers 53, 60–1

Gisborne 47–8
Glendhu Bay 89
Greymouth 61-2

Hamilton 28–9
Hastings 49, 50
health matters 120
history of New Zealand
  8–11
Hokitika 62
Howick Colonial
  Village 21
Hutt Valley 43

Invercargill 78-9, *79*

Kaikoura 62–3
Kapiti Coast 43
Karangahake Gorge 35
Kauaeranga Valley 34–5
Kelly Tarlton's
  Underwater World 17
Kerikeri 27

language 126
Larnach Castle 72
Little Barrier Island
  91–2
local etiquette 108–10

local time 125
lost property 120

Manapouri 79, 80
Maori people *8*, 8–9,
  10, 12, *13*, *32*, *105*,
  108-9
maps
  Auckland Environs
    18-19
  Central New Zealand
    40 1
  Christchurch
    Environs 56–7
  Dunedin Environs
    70–1
  New Zealand 5, 7
  The Northern Region
    14–15
  Northland 26
  South Island: The
    North 64-5
  South Island: The
    South 74–5
  Wellington 44-5
Marine Drive 42
Marlborough Sounds
  67
Masterton *48*, 48–9
media 121
Milford Sound *11*, 69,
  81, 81–2, 97
Milford Track *80–1*, 82
Mona Vale 55
money 121
Mount Aspiring National
  Park *89*, 89, 96
Mount Cargill 73, *76*
Mount Cavandish
  Gondola 55
Mount Cook 7, 82–3
Mount Cook National
  Park 69, 96
Mount Eden 17–18
Mount Egmont 39, 50,
  50–1, 51
Mount Maunganui 34
Mount Victoria 42
Museum of New
  Zealand 42
Museum of Transport
  and Technology 20

Napier 49, 50
National Archives 42
National Library of New
  Zealand 42

INDEX/ACKNOWLEDGEMENTS

Nelson 63, *66*, 66–7, 94–5
New Plymouth 60 1
Ninety Mile Beach 13, 28
North Island 6, 13–52

Oamaru 83–4
Ohinemutu 30
Olveston 72, *72*
opening times 122
Orana Wildlife Park 55
Orewa 20–1
Otago Early Settlers Museum 72
Otago Museum 72
Otago Peninsula 72–3

Paihia 26
Palmerston North 51–2
Pancake Rocks 62, *62–3*
Parliament Buildings 42–3, *43*
passports /visas 115–16
personal safety 116, 122
Picton *67*, 67–8
Piha 21
places of worship 122
police 122
post offices 123
public holidays 120
public transport 111, 123–4

Queenstown 69, 84–7, *84, 85, 86*

Rangitoto Island 16, 21
restaurants 99–100 (see also individual locations)
Rotorua 6, 29–32, *30–1*, 92
Russell 25–6

senior citizens 124
shopping 101-3
Shotover River *69*, 85-6
Skippers Canyon 85
South Island 6, 53–89
sport and leisure activities 36, 113–14
Stewart Island 6, 69, 87, 97–8
student and youth travel 124–5

Taiaroa Head 73, 95
Taieri Gorge 73
Tasman Glacier 82–3
Taupo 32–3, *93*
Tauranga 33–4
Te Anau 79–80, 97
telephones 125
Te Urewera National Park 92–3
Thames 34
Tikitere 30
Timaru 87–8

tipping 110, 125
toilets 125
Tongariro National Park 35–6, *36*, 92
tourist offices 125–6
travel agents 126

voltage 119

Waimangu 30
Waipoua Forest Sanctuary 36–7
Wairakei Geothermal Power Station 32–3
Waitangi 26–7
Waitomo Caves 37
Wanaka 88–9
Wanganui 52
Wellington 4, *38–9*, 39–47, 93–4
Westland National Park 53, 96
Westport 68
Whakapapa Village 36
Whakarewarewa Thermal Reserve 30
Whakatane 37
Whanganui River 52
Whangarei 38
Whitianga 35

youth hostels 124–5

Zoo (Auckland) 20

The Automobile Association would like to thank the following photographers, libraries and associations for their assistance in the preparation of this book.

PAUL KENWARD who took all the photographs in this book not listed below
MARY EVANS PICTURE LIBRARY 8 Hongi Ika.
NATURE PHOTOGRAPHERS LTD 92 Tuatara (S C Bisserott), 94 Little blue penguins (M P Harris), 95 Royal albatross (M P Harris), 97 New Zealand blue duck (P R Sterry).
NEW ZEALAND TOURISM OFFICE 20 Narrow Neck Beach Devonport, 22 Regent of Auckland, 29 Cape Reinga, 34/5 Coromandel Peninsula, 36 Tongariro N. Park, 43 Parliament building Wellington, 47 Cable cars Wellington City, 50/1 Farmstead Mt Egmont, 55 Cathedral Sq Christchurch, 66 Trafalgar St Nelson, 71 Otago University Dunedin,, 76 Harbour View Mt Cargill, 78 Oysters, 80/1 Milford Track, 89 Mt Aspiring, 93 Kowhai Tree, 96 Kiwi, 99 Hangi, 101 Food, 114 Yachting Lyttelton Harbour, 124 Craftshop.
SPECTRUM COLOUR LIBRARY Cover Mount Cook, 38/9 Wellington, 48 Pool Masterton.
ZEFA PICTURE LIBRARY UK LTD 11 Milford Sound, 79 Invercargill.

Thanks also to **Allan Edie**, the **New Zealand Automobile Association** and the **New Zealand Tourism Board** (London) for their assistance in updating this revised edition.

Copy editor for original edition: Audrey Horne
For this revision: Copy editor Jenny Fry; verifier Colin Follett